Cross

Over

The New Model for Youth Basketball Development

A resource for players, parents and coaches

By Brian McCormick, M.S.S., CSCS

Printed and bound in the United States of America

Cover design: John Hayashi / Inkblot Creative Asylum /inkblot.ca@gmail.com

Thank you to my trusty editors, Thomas McCormick III and Brianna Finch.

Other Books published by Brian McCormick:

The Art of Ball Handling; Getting a Handle on Your Game

Pure: The Biomechanics and Mental Approach to Successful Shooting

Hard 2 Guard: The Fundamental Skills of the Unstoppable Perimeter Player

Available from Basketball Sense publication: www.basketballsense.com

Contents

Section I

The Introduction to 21st Century Basketball in the United States

Section II

The New Model for Long Term Basketball Development in the United States

Section III

Beyond the School System: A Proposal for Elite Player Development

Section IV

Dedication

This book is dedicated to all the coaches who worked with me as a youth: Rita Gifford, Bill McDevitt, Mike Shulters, Dan Vistica, Steve Fahey, Steve Morrison, Claude Moore, Steve Williams, Jim McCaslin, Jim Peth, and, most importantly, my dad, who managed to coach or assist with almost every team.

I would also like to thank all the coaches who have impacted my coaching career, beliefs and philosophy: Lauren Kelly, Jerome Green, Ahmad Clayton, Dante Sarmiento, Oscar Lopez-Borbon, John Hayashi, Veronica Jordan, Thierry Kita, Craig Daniels, Rick Allison, Lindell Singleton, Clay Kallam, Dave Hopla, Rick Majerus, Lute Olson, Josh Pastner, Vance Walberg, Mark Grabow, Eric Bridgeland, Patrick Pavelchik, and, most significantly, Brianna Finch.

Finally, to all the players who made me step-up my game, especially Matt Glynn, Johanna Ericsson, Ryan Sypkens and "my boys" Branden, Miracle, Allen, Ray and the entire UCLA Special Olympics family.

In a 2002 letter to the editor of *Basketball Times*, I wrote:

> America has an embarrassment of riches; however, the richness creates problems. The star system, the one-on-one games, the lack of real skill development, the AAU coaches who roll out the ball are part of the problem, though they pat each other on the back for the successes. For every T-Mac created by the ABCD Camp, how many players are built up to the point that they lose sight of the work ethic and the fundamentals that helped them reach that point? While American basketball remains head and shoulders above the world at large, elite players have closed the gap, as evidenced by this summer's World Championships and the prevalence of so many international players in the L. America must realize that one-on-one skill can take a player only so far; players must learn to play the game on both ends of the court, inside and outside, with and without the ball.

However, not until the 2004 Olympics did basketball personnel and the media truly recognize the problem and begin assessing the damages. Unfortunately, the changes are short-sighted, focused entirely on the 2006 World Championships and 2008 Olympics with little thought to the future of the game. USA Basketball aims to remedy problems at the top, influencing the Olympic team and possibly the NBA; however, true change, real improvement starts at the bottom, in the pivotal years of development when young athletes are ten to twelve years old.

The following provides a model for youth development based on those used throughout the world. These ideas challenge the American status quo and argue for change in the way we as a society approach youth sports, coaching and elite player development. From my experience, I believe youth sport suffers from a myriad of problems. The following is an attempt to emphasize the important aspects of sports (teamwork, fun, learning, self-confidence), while providing a framework for development to maximize the talent and experiences of every athlete whether recreational or elite.

Practice in Proportion to your Aspirations

Chapter 1:
The Current Basketball System

The current approach to basketball development in the United States squeezes the recreational and developmental athletes, while failing to transition competitive and developmental athletes into elite performers. At every level of participation, four categories of athletes exist and all athletes possess characteristics of each: Recreational, Developmental, Competitive and Elite.

Recreational athletes dominate either end of the age spectrum, either novice players or weekend warriors. Fun and exercise motivate recreational athletes; training is not extensive, as play is most important. *Developmental* athletes are common throughout the four stages. Skill acquisition, learning and improvement motivate developmental athletes, and they use competition to measure their progress, not determine their rank.

Competitive athletes take the game seriously, train on and off the court and compete to win and continue their career. Most athletes progress naturally from the Developmental to Competitive level around fourteen to sixteen years old. However, if an athlete is too competitive too early, he peaks, stunts his basketball development and hinders his athletic enjoyment. *Elite* athletes arise mainly toward the end of high school, though some players blossom early; elite athletes possess college and professional potential and ability. They manifest similar characteristics to the competitive athlete, but their overall talent exceeds their peers. Elite athletes require special nurturing to maximize their ability.

The current state of basketball development in the United States overemphasizes competitive characteristics and ignores developmental and recreational characteristics. Even the development of elite athletes suffers from the lack of preparation and gradual development before athletes train to win. Children are not miniature adults; however, the current youth sports system imposes adult training protocols on youths, ignoring the important physiological development stages each child enters and passes through during childhood. Instead of appreciating the needs of young athletes, the sports society is in hyper-drive, as adidas offers exposure camps for ten year olds so national ranking services like Hoop Scoop Online can rank the top 4th graders in the country.

The hyper-competitive atmosphere hampers elite player development from the player's initial participation with an organized team or league. Typically, a child joins a sports team or league because he demonstrates an affinity and an aptitude for the sport in an informal environment, whether shooting baskets in his front yard or playing basketball at recess. The child's interest is motivated by play, moving around, fun and friends. However, once on a formal team, many of these motivations disappear, as coaches teach players to work hard, instilling the great American virtue; work and fun are incompatible in most coaches' eyes.

When players move to formal teams, whether school teams, recreation leagues or AAU/club teams, two problems occur: (1) The game changes from a player-directed, informal, fun environment to an adult-centered, competition-based atmosphere centered on game preparation; and (2) Basketball-specific activities replace general games like tag, chasing the dog and riding bikes.

The shift from play to competition and general to sport-specific hinders athletic development on two levels:

(1) At the recreation level-players interested in fun and exercise- play is lost and fun disappears; practice is work and running (the most basic movement skill and foundation for almost all sports) is associated with punishment. In games, some kids do not play much or at all and one star dominates the ball. Coaches implore players to run the play, a euphemism for "do exactly what I say with no deviation or thinking on your part or you are going to sit on the bench." For many children, the experience differs from the joy experienced playing basketball on the playground or in the neighborhood, and they quit formal basketball. Some return to the innocence of games in their neighborhood, but some dislike the experience so greatly they quit sports altogether. Sports sociologist Jay Coakley (Sport in Society) reports that twelve is the peak age for sports participation. By thirteen years old, most athletes specialize in one sport (thus lowering participation figures) or quit and seek another after-school activity.

(2) The immediate competitive play emphasis, termed the "Peak by Friday" mentality by Dr. Istvan Balyi, ignores important preparation and development stages which lead to better performance and overall ability as the athlete grows. For purposes of developing elite players, the early competition and focus on winning inhibits well-rounded skill development. Peak by Friday coaches do not have time to insure players move correctly, learn to run and jump with proper form or perform dynamic warm-up activities because they have too much to do to prepare for the next game. However, how many teams struggle because a player is out with an ACL injury or an overuse injury like shin splints, tendonitis or plantar fasciitis? How many players develop poor shooting mechanics to compensate for poor general movement skills? How many teams perform optimally in a certain defense if the players are not as fast, quick or agile as possible? An athlete with poorly developed general athletic ability never reaches his/her peak because every sport-specific skill builds upon a general athletic skill, whether manipulative (throwing), loco motor (running), non-loco motor (balancing) or movement awareness (visual awareness).

The pre-professional environment inhibits elite and non-elite athletes. The sport loses athletes because sport is too competitive before the athlete is developmentally ready for the competition and many athletes progress with poorly developed movement skills which eventually stalls the athlete's development and causes the athlete to reach a premature peak and plateau, as opposed to continuing to develop and improve throughout the duration of the athlete's career. A student cannot progress and excel in more rigorous studies without the ability to read and write; similarly, general movement skills provide the foundation for any sport, and an athlete is unprepared for more rigorous training without these skills.

The irony of the United States youth basketball player is so many players and parents exist in an atmosphere with one eye firmly fixed on the future, yet nobody appropriately plans or organizes long term athlete development (LTAD). Playing basketball is no longer an end; it is merely a vehicle to a college scholarship. The 'ship, in many circles, is the impetus, not a reward for the talented player. No longer is the journey the destination; now, one must reach a tangible destination (worth six figures) to justify play. While other countries organize and embrace LTAD plans, United States basketball exists in a vacuum, with players going season to season, team to team and coach to coach with eyes fixed on the prize, but no plan to get there. Nowhere is the future so omnipresent in players' minds, yet nowhere is less emphasis given to the path to the desired destination. The entire American basketball system epitomizes John Wooden's refrain: "Failing to prepare is preparing to fail."

In the European club system, players progress from age group to age group, eventually to the professional level; many clubs feature reserve teams or lower division adult teams for players too old for the youth programs but not good enough for the top team. Most players develop within one club from youth to the professional level; if the player is unable to make the professional side, he may transfer to another club; or, if supremely talented, he may transfer to a more prestigious domestic club, transfer to a team in a better league (from Slovenia to Spain for instance) or even enter the NBA draft. The process builds to a peak in the player's early twenties when he is playing professionally.

The American model achieves maximum results in high school; many talented girls peak around their sophomore year of *high school*, while many boys peak before they matriculate to college. I followed a talented AAU team from 8th to 12th grade; of the seven players, three quit before their senior year of high school, one verballed to a Division I school, one received interest from NAIA schools but decided not to play, one is a high school senior and one is unknown: for all but one player, the peak of her career was 8th or 9th grade. Training to win at a premature age leads to the early peak as players rush the developmental process.

Our priorities differ from European clubs. European clubs exist to perform and produce a product which draws fans, sponsors and ultimately money; the best method to insure consistent performance is to develop one's own players through the youth program. In the United States, coaches gain little through a long term approach, as a player is likely to play with a new coach during the next season. Many recreation leagues draft new teams for each season; AAU teams operate on a season-to-season basis, except for the rare few; high school players typically play for three coaches (Freshman, Junior Varsity and Varsity) in four years. Not until college is there significant continuity. If a youth coach prepares a player for continued development and success, but loses his games, he is judged by his win-loss record; if the player eventually earns a scholarship or plays professionally, the youth coach sees no reward or gets no credit. We evaluate coaches solely on won/loss record, so coaches speed the development curve to win at their level.

In the USA, the Amateur Athletic Union (AAU) crowns an u-9 National Champion; in Canada, basketball players do not start 5-on-5 competition until 12 years of age; in Italy, "junior teams start at age six, but can't play in competitions until age 10. Once you reach age 12, you can play for real," says Enrico Castorina (Kravitz). Research suggests nine year olds play a wide array of activities to challenge and develop multilateral skills in a fun, playful atmosphere (think recess, kickball, dodgeball, tag, etc) rather than compete for national championships.

"This is the narrow approach applied to children's sports, in which the only scope of training is achieving quick results, irrespective of what may happen in the future of the young athlete. In their attempt to achieve the fast results, coaches expose children to highly specific and intensive training without taking the time to build a good base. This is like trying to build a high rise building on a poor foundation. Obviously, such a construction error will result in the collapse of the building. Likewise, encouraging athletes to narrowly focus on their development in one sport before they are ready physically and psychologically often leads to problems," (Bompa).

According to NCAA statistics, 1-3% of high school basketball players play NCAA basketball. Parents, players and coaches see these facts, and the competitive nature of youth sports, and believe the best opportunity to secure one of the coveted scholarships is to start playing before other kids, to specialize in basketball before other kids, to use a personal trainer more often than other kids, to go to more camps than other kids. An entire childhood is spent competing against a statistic in order to procure a college scholarship; unfortunately, for many players reared in this environment, the last thing they want is to play another four years of overly structured basketball which dominates their entire life and takes on the commitment level and pressure of a full-time job.

Instead of forfeiting childhood in the pursuit of the elusive free ride, these statistics should humble parents. While every child should be encouraged to dream big and pursue his/her dream, the dream should be the child's own; when parents of eight year olds call to set-up personal training appointments, I doubt the child is behind the dream, sitting at the dinner table asking his parents for a personal trainer so he can step-up his game at recess. Rather than embark on a single-minded mission to get a college scholarship, parents, coaches and players should embrace the fun and life lessons of sports and appreciate the opportunity to play. In the process of focusing on the fun and learning inherent in the challenge of the activity, athletes develop better and broader skills. If the player has a happy confluence of work ethic, genetics, opportunity and skills, he/she may conquer the scholarship quest; however, if not, the athlete will lead a happier childhood with a greater appreciation for sports and a more well-rounded set of athletic skills.

Chapter 2:
The Problem with Early Specialization

The NCAA statistics warn athletes, parents and coaches of the scholarships' quest steep odds, yet athletes specialize in one sport earlier and earlier. Few high school athletes play three sports; many ten to twelve year old children choose (or have a sport chosen) to specialize in only one sport, ignoring other recreational and formal opportunities to focus solely on basketball. Coaches, to a large degree, encourage specialization; high school programs run practices and compete in tournaments year-round and expect players to participate. Some coaches believe playing another sport retards the athlete's basketball development, though these assessments could not be further from the truth. The current popular belief that a player must specialize in his/her chosen sport before the end of puberty is a myth perpetrated by coaches and trainers who profit from training players and operating off-season leagues and tournaments.

Furthermore, considering less than 3% of high school basketball players continue their competitive careers beyond high school, what do children gain through specialization? For the elite, college-bound athlete, a greater emphasis in one sport may serve a purpose; however, ironically, the college-bound athletes are often the ones playing more than one sport because they are the best athletes and excel in a wide variety of sports, leaving the lesser athletes to specialize in one sport in a fleeting attempt to catch the multi-sport star.

Early specialization-before the end of puberty-hinders athletic and social development in four ways:

First, playing multiple sports or engaging in multiple activities increases an athlete's multilateral development. Multilateral training is a philosophy to develop bio-motor qualities in planned balance which is essential to long term success; the bio-motor qualities are Strength, Speed, Endurance, Flexibility and Coordination. A strong, balanced foundation of these qualities enhances performance in any sport. "When we are talking about kids, tag may just be the greatest game ever invented…There is linear speed, lateral speed, angular take offs, moving backwards, avoidance skills, cutting, change of direction, faking skills, breaking down skills, reaching skills, body control skills, balance, flexibility, coordination, raising and lowering of the center of mass, setting up opponents, strategies, team work…Basically tag will force you to reach deep into the movement bag of tricks your body has stored, or better yet, not stored and force you to use it or learn it," (Taft).

By simply playing, athletes develop many of the general skills needed for advanced sports participation. Playing baseball enhances hand-eye coordination; playing soccer trains endurance; playing football increases strength and speed; playing tennis increases coordination and speed; playing water polo increases strength and endurance. Athletes who only play basketball develop with a more shallow foundation and eventually require remedial training to develop broader, general skills; also, the repetitive movements of one sport can lead to muscle imbalances and tightness, which decreases flexibility and performance. Youth Development Specialist Brian Grasso says, "In fact, between the ages of 6 – 14, athletes should be focused primarily on developing fundamental proficiency in as many athletic skills as possible. Running, jumping, throwing, lateral movement, spatial orientation – the list is long and endless. The fundamental components of ANY sport are based on movement ability and associated physical properties, such as summation of forces and neuromuscular sequencing. Athletes must progressively master the science of movement as children, (Grasso).

Second, playing multiple sports creates a natural periodization for athletes. Periodization is the process of planning training to peak for important games or competitions. Coaches plan using macro, micro and meso cycles to break the year and training into different parts to insure adaptation to the training, but also prevent overtraining, which leads to performance decreases. For young athletes, multiple sports create a natural periodization, and the athlete concentrates on each sport during its season and builds from the pre-season through the season and peaks in the post-season.

Third, playing multiple sports reduces the incidence of overuse injuries such as tendonitis, plantar fasciitis and shin splints; the number of adolescent overuse injuries has increased dramatically in the past ten years as more and more athletes specialize in one sport. The American Academy of Pediatrics, advises that "youngsters should be discouraged from specializing in a single sport before adolescence to avoid physical and psychological damage. The risks range from 'overuse' injuries such as stress fractures to delayed menstruation, eating disorders, emotional stress and burnout." Athletes undergo tremendous repetitive stress on muscles, joints and ligaments unprepared for the year-round training. Without a gradual progression from general to specific and a complimentary conditioning program to balance bio-motor training, athletes' bodies stop working properly and the breakdown manifests itself as an overuse injury.

While playing multiple sports prolongs athletic demands and training stress, the change in environment and activity reduces stress. For basketball players, constant running and jumping on hardwood floors is hard on the body, especially the knee and ankle joint. Playing a season of soccer or football dissipates the stress because the grass is easier on the joints; playing baseball alleviates much of the repetitive stress because it reduces the running volume. Using muscles in different environments and actions prevents the muscle imbalances and tightness which cause many of the overuse injuries; plantar fasciitis is caused, in part, by tightness in the gastroc soleus (calf) and Achilles tendon. Tightness in the calf is usually associated with weakness in its antagonist, or the tibialis anterior (shin); playing soccer, as opposed to year-round basketball, may decrease the weakness in the tibialis anterior due to the kicking exercises in soccer.

Finally, playing multiple sports is fun and engages young athletes in multiple activities with different teammates, coaches and social environments. When players play close to one hundred basketball games a year, the importance of an individual game is lost and the player is fatigued mentally and physically. Almost everyone who covers high school AAU basketball notices the precipitous drop in play during the last week of the summer evaluation periods, as players basically go non-stop from September through the end of July and are burnt out psychologically, as well as physically. As one WCC women's assistant coach said to me: "I think burnout is a problem because the kids play too many summer games. Also, injuries occur because a lot of teams do not take breaks during the summer recruiting period."

With little to gain through early specialization, why are parents, coaches and young athletes in such a hurry to rush the developmental process? Presently, most athletes stop playing sports by eighteen years old, as only the elite few play competitively in college.

However, why accept the end of high school as the end of play? Some participate in college intramurals and adult recreation leagues; however, others simply stop playing sports altogether. At its most basic level, youth sports provide a foundation for athletic participation throughout one's life; a multilateral approach to training prepares young athletes for athletic participation in a variety of activities throughout their lifetime.

Unfortunately, the 1% motivates coaches, parents and players to specialize and give the athlete the "best" opportunity to achieve his goal. Ironically, the approach has the opposite effect, as early specialization leads to injury, psychological burnout or stunted athletic development. "In 1985, a study by the Swedish Tennis Association suggested that early specialization is unnecessary for players to achieve high performance levels in tennis. Among other things, this study found that the players who were part of the Swedish tennis 'miracle' of the 1980s, including the great Bjorn Borg, were keenly active in a range of sports until the age of 14 and did not begin to specialize until about the age of 16," (Launder).

Playing numerous sports develops a wide array of skills which ultimately leads to enhanced performance when the athlete specializes. Early specialization leads to early sport-specific development and immediate performance gains; however, early peaks accompany the early development, and over the course of one's athletic career, the early specialization has a detrimental effect. In the Swedish study, "what was most significant was that many players who had been superior to the eventual elite while in the 12-14 age group had dropped out-been burned out-of the sport," (Launder).

Chapter 3:
The Disappearance of Unstructured Play

Few things are as enjoyable as watching kids at play (or being a kid at play). When I coached an u-9 AAU team with the Hoop Masters program in West Los Angeles, two boys played and battled each other after every practice. Invariably, their parents would stand around talking and they would play 1v1 in the hallway or on the sidewalk, looking to dribble around each other or through the others legs. They were kids playing around having fun. And, the 1v1 play hastened their skill development.

I coached the team with Ahmad Clayton and Jerome Green; we managed, at once, to keep the atmosphere fun for the players and have opposing parents remark positively about the skill level and discipline of the players. Rather than using boring drills to improve their ball handling, Ahmad played follow the leader, incorporating tricks and fancy dribbles into the fundamentals to keep the drill fun; rather than allot most of practice to drills, Jerome implored us to scrimmage. Through the fun, competitive drills and small-sided games, players improved their skills and ability; we won tournaments though we never practiced against zones, never ran a shell drill, had only one basic offensive set, one out of bounds play and no real press break. Instead, we had aggressive players who could handle the ball, pass and defend the ball. We embraced unstructured play, added basic instruction and watched the players flourish.

Children repeatedly offer four major reasons for quitting organized sports: (1) Practice is boring (too many drills); (2) Emotional stress from excessive performance demands (too focused on winning too early); (3) Feelings of constant failure, typically due to negative coaching; and (4) Not playing enough. None of these problems occur in informal settings, when the action is child or player-directed; however, once adults intervene, and structure is added, the best elements of sports are lost.

I am an avid reader; I read anything and everything. However, as a high school junior, my English teacher asked, "Why do you hate English?" In college, I almost never finished an assigned book though I was an American Literature major. When I was told what to read and how to read it (too many drills), with expectations of an exam (performance demands), and received critical comments on my writing (negative coaching) in a large class without individual attention or instruction (playing time), my motivation to read decreased and I derived very little pleasure from the books. However, upon graduation, when I was free to choose what books I read for my own purposes, I enjoyed reading, was motivated to read more and learned more as a result. The educational process dampened my enjoyment and my learning, while the freedom to explore expanded my horizons and encouraged my self-awakening.

According to Sport Sociologist Jay Coakley, "Childhood has been changed from an age of exploration and freedom to an age of preparation and controlled learning." Furthermore, "playing informal sports clearly involves the use of interpersonal and decision-making skills. Children must be creative to organize games and keep them going," while "organized sports demand that children be able to manage their relationships with adult authority figures," (Coakley). In organized sports, prized players follow directions; in informal play, children create their own rules and games.

Children play sports for fun, to move around and to be amongst friends; however, most coaches and leagues ignore these basic principles. In some cases, it appears coaches go out of their way to insure practices are not fun, as coaches equate fun with laughing and lackadaisical, while children equate fun with play, challenges and movement. Children identify with the innocence and fun of the And 1 Mix-Tapes, especially in contradiction to their typically boring, overly structured practices governed by rule after rule. The Mix-Tapes destroy the status quo and break the rules if necessary to increase the fun or challenge; typical practices stifle challenges and fun through continuous, repetitive drilling and/or running.

Informal play in my childhood meant games of HORSE or 3v3 to 15 or 5v5 to 11; it meant games at recess and lunch. These games taught valuable skills, such as how to get open against bigger, stronger players; how to make three-pointers to avoid going in amongst much bigger, older kids; how to shoot lay-ups from different angles over and around bigger players; and how to make left-handed hook shots to win games of HORSE with my neighbor. Playing was a time for exploration, to try new skills, to imitate more skilled players and invent my own moves. Without a fear of failure or need to impress a coach, I played with freedom; a freedom and joy the high school coaches aimed to silence through the five-pass rule and other means to control the action from the sideline. While many coaches criticize the And 1 Tapes, nothing ruined basketball for me like the overly structured, over-coached high school basketball.

The current pre-professional environment ignores basic physical fitness for all youths and leaves basic motor skills untaught as young athletes pursue advanced sport-specific skills. While ignoring basic, general athletic concepts, the hyper-intensive environment chases many children away from sports. Kenyan distance runners are among the most dominant athletes in sports. However, they do not overcomplicate training; they run because they love to run. "Kenyan runners, instead of pushing themselves until they are uncomfortable, use comfort and enjoyment as the key to the success. With enjoyment as their bottom line, performance unfolds gracefully. Loving what they do gives them a built-in desire to train. Their outstanding achievements are more a side effect of enjoyment than the result of an obsession to win," (Douillard).

While researching youth sports on the Internet, I saw an advertisement for fundamental skills workouts for eight year olds, not to mention several AAU teams championing the exploits of their eight-and-under teams. My personal feeling is eight year olds should not even play organized sports; they should be immersed in playful activities, swim lessons, martial arts, group games, tag, bike riding and other activities. Developing proper basketball fundamentals should not be an issue for an eight year old. However, youth sports increasingly move away from free play, as more and more play activities are adult-centered and structured. For numerous reasons-safety, convenience, competition-parents seek organized, supervised play experiences for their children; however, these play experiences typically lose the playful nature and engage in competition almost immediately. These are not child-centered activities where a child leaves his house, finds some neighbors and creates a game in the street; these are formal sports leagues directed by adults telling children exactly what to do. And, following an adult's directions is never as fun as creating one's own activity without interference.

Every player deserves the right to play. In elementary and middle school, we played 6v6 or 7v7 at recess because that's how many boys wanted to play and we only had one court; now, a smarter use of court space may have been to play half court 3v3 games so everyone got the ball more, but we were eleven years old and wanted to run up and down the court after sitting in our small desks for the entire morning. We found a way to make it work. When I lived in Sweden as an exchange student and played for the local club, I coached an u-14 boy's team. I started with 8-10 players and slowly but surely, more and more players attended. At the peak, we had 26 players for a practice. I never told anyone to leave; it was an inconvenience, but if they were willing to walk through the snow to get to practice, I was going teach them something and make it a fun experience, even though I spoke little Swedish and they spoke little English.

Everyone wants to be involved, to be a part of the action. Is it any wonder the kid standing out in right field quits playing? After all, isn't that the subconscious reason the coach consistently puts him there? Why would a child play a sport when he isn't really playing? At least with a video game he is visually stimulated.

Again, the key word for youth sports is PLAY. Kids need the opportunity to run around, explore, learn, develop and have fun. Play, as defined by Webster's –n. 1. Motion or activity, esp. when free or rapid; 2. Freedom for motion or action; 3. Recreation or sport; 4. Fun; joking; 5. The playing of a game. More play is the first step toward redefining the American youth sports culture.

Beyond issues of fun, play, creativity, imagination and self-reliance, the shift shortchanges the learning environment within the competitive sports arena. "At least two recent studies have confirmed that informal play and practice are important elements in the development of elite players, and little doubt exists that informal pick-up game have been critical in the development of many great players," (Launder).

Every great American basketball icon developed, at least in part, on a playground or schoolyard; in fact, the recent stumbles in the 2002 World Championships and 2004 Olympics result more from a lack of instinctive, creative play than the typical criticisms of selfishness and poor fundamentals. While American players once distinguished themselves internationally because of the feel for the game, their creativity and instinctive play, current professional players develop in an overly structured and star-driven system; while exceptional athletes and remarkable on-ball players, the feel for the game disappears annually as the game, at all levels, increases in structure. According to the *Journal of Experimental Psychology: Applied*, athletes who learn the intricacies of a game on their own perform better than those who are heavily coached. As playground and schoolyard basketball is associated with the And 1 Tapes, and thus discourgaed by coaches and parents, fewer players learn these intricacies on their own,which means fewer players possess the feel for the game.

This informal learning is not just for advanced or seasoned players; "Beginners…usually have little to no idea where defenders should be…So when they move from drill to game, the intervention of defenders often causes them to forget everything they have learned," (Launder). The use of small-sided games as a teaching tool is more effective as more players stay involved in the action, players learn in a game-like situation, more players get touches and players have more fun than standing around doing boring drills. Also, athletes learn better when they control their learning.

Without elements of play, whether on the playground or at practice, basketball loses its fun and over-coaching stifles elite player development. To improve basketball at the recreational through elite levels, coaches and parents must embrace play and celebrate the fun and challenge of basketball development, not over-think the process.

Chapter 4:
The Need for a Better Model: Long Term Athlete Development Introduced

When the United States lost in 2002 and 2004 at the World Championships and Olympics, the media criticized NBA players and USA Basketball's selection process. While arguments raged over whether Kobe Bryant was selfish for skipping the Olympics or whether Stephon Marbury was a good fit for International basketball, few discussed other nation's ability to close the talent and competitive gap and nobody mentioned the declining development system feeding players to the NBA.

While the United States maintains a helter-skelter development system with no unifying organization, other countries develop players through their club system and national programs. Players play for the youth program affiliated with a professional club from the time they start playing, and the club guides development to insure a constant influx of talent to the professional team. National programs use the youth club programs to identify talented players with National Team potential and run camps and training for these players. While competition and championships exist for youth age groups, the primary purpose for these clubs is to develop players for the professional side, so wins and losses at the youth level are not emphasized. While it appears to be a contradiction, the professionalized development model used in Europe is more athlete-centered than the current hodge-podge of programs offered in the United States.

In the United States, no long term development plan exists and players jump from team to team and coach to coach annually, until the varsity high school level, where a player may spend 2-4 years with the same team and coach, though different teammates. Throughout this development, each coach uses his own philosophy and each team trains to win its championship. In this model, winning, not long term development is valued, often sacrificing an athlete's development for the best opportunity to win.

What is Long Term Athlete Development?

The European club model creates a unified approach to train and develop players, while in the USA, teams exist for one season. Each system has inherent advantages; however, the club model offers distinct advantages for player development because of the cooperation between coaches and the long term development emphasis for the professional club's benefit.

In the United States, little cooperation exists between coaches. In high school, club teams and school teams battle for players' time and allegiance, rather than working together for the athlete's benefit. In the European club system, professional coaches direct the overall development of the youth clubs and coaches work together, sharing insight, working with players, etc. Russian coaches criticize the American system because American coaches only work with one development level; Russian coaches work simultaneously with more than one development level, insuring they understand the skills youth players need to advance.

When I coached professionally in Sweden, I assisted with an u-11, u-13 and u-15 team. Training prepared the next generation of professional players and developed the skills required to compete at the professional level. For many clubs, the professional team's lifeblood is the youth programs' ability to develop talent. In the United States, no unifying system exists; the Los Angeles Lakers have no stake in the development of young basketball players from the Challenger's Boys and Girls Club, Manual Arts High School, Long Angeles Trade Tech or USC, all located in the shadows of the Staples Center. If these programs fail to develop the next generation, the Lakers look elsewhere.

While not perfect, the European club system promotes Long Term Athlete Development (LTAD). LTAD is a model created by Dr. Istvan Balyi to guide the athletic development process from pre-puberty through retirement; his work is used by national sports governing bodies and professional clubs throughout the world.

Balyi's Late Specialization Model

Stage 1: **The FUNdamental Stage**
Age: Males 6-9/Females 6-8 years
Objective: Learn all fundamental movement skills (build overall motor skills)
Participation once or twice per week [in desired sport], but participation in other sports three or four times per week is essential for further excellence.

Stage 2: **The Learning to Train Stage**
Age: Males 9-12/Females 8-11 years
Objective: Learn all fundamental sports skills (build overall sports skills)
A 70:30 training/practice to competition ratio is recommended.

Stage 3: **The Training to Train Stage**
Age: Males 12-16/Females 11-15 years
Objectives: Build the aerobic base, build strength towards the end of the phase and further develop sport-specific skills (build the "engine" and consolidate sport-specific skills)
60 percent training to 40 percent competition ratio is recommended by experts…and the 40 percent competition ratio includes competition and competition-specific training.

Stage 4: **The Training to Compete Stage**
Age: Males 16-18/Females 15-17 years
Objectives: Optimize fitness preparation and sport, individual and position-specific skills as well as performance (optimize "engine," skills and performance)
The training to competition and competition-specific training ratio now changes to 50:50. Fifty percent of available time is devoted to the development of technical and tactical skills and fitness improvements and fifty percent is devoted to competition and competition-specific training.

Stage 5: **The Training to Win Stage**
Age: Males 18+/Females 17+
Objectives: Maximize fitness preparation and sport, individual and position-specific skills as well as performance (maximize "engine", skills and performance)
Training to competition ratio in this phase is 25:75, with the competition percentage including competition-specific training activities.

Stage 6: **The Retirement/Retention Stage**
Objectives: Retain athletes for coaching, administration, officials, etc.

(Balyi and Hamilton, 2003)

Scientific research concludes "it takes eight-to-twelve years of training for a talented player/athlete to reach elite levels. This is called the ten-year or 10,000 hour rule," (Balyi and Hamilton, 2003). However, despite the necessary time commitment, and the long path to greatness, "parents and coaches in many sports still approach training with an attitude best characterized as 'peaking by Friday,' where short-term approach is taken to training and performance with an over-emphasis on immediate results," (Balyi and Hamilton, 2003).

With a long term approach, shooting instruction is easy, as a player takes his time learning proper form from a comfortable distance without pressure to perform; however, when a player has an up-coming game and pressure to win, shooting form disappears, as the player bombs away.

A *Peak by Friday* coach ignores basics such as general movement skills and a gradual progression of skills. Instead of teaching proper running stride or how to bend one's knees properly, the coach teaches several set plays and a press break to organize his team for the up coming game. While these lessons have their place, the ability to move supercedes all basketball-specific skills. The emphasis, at young ages, is totally reversed, as the "little things" are far more important to the player's future development than mastery of additional plays.

The "Peak by Friday" mentality stifles individual development because "overemphasizing competition in the early phases of training will always cause shortcomings in athletic abilities later in an athlete's career," (Balyi and Hamilton, 2003). If players never achieve a base level of athleticism, their athletic career ends prematurely. When I was young, my technical basketball skills surpassed nearly every player I faced; however, I never learned to move laterally or squat properly and consequently my career ended earlier than my technical and tactical skills warranted because of insufficient athleticism.

The opposite of the "Peak by Friday" mentality is not a total abdication of competitive play or the desire to win. Instead, the LTAD model proposes a more balanced approach: players play to win, however, training is directed towards development. Teach basic skills like lateral movement, ball handling, shooting form, etc. with some practice time devoted to game preparation. Encourage the team to play hard and attempt to win, but the win is not the end-goal: developing players for the next level is the ultimate goal and wins are a by-product. "The reason why so many athletes plateau during the later stages of their careers is primarily because of an overemphasis on competition instead of training during the important period in their athletic development. The "Learn to Train" and "Training to Train" stages are the most important phases of athletic preparation. During these stages, we make or break an athlete," (Balyi and Hamilton, 2003).

Young students learn a foreign language easier and quicker than adults because the child's mind is "ripe" for learning. Sensitive periods of athletic development also exist; teaching young athletes these skills at the appropriate ages enhances their development.

Girls	Item	Boys
9-10	Balance	10-11
8-13	Movement Adequacy	8-13
6-7 & 10-11	Kinesthetic Differentiation	6-7 & 10-11
8-10	Reaction to Acoustical & visual signals	8-10
7-9	Rhythmic Motion	9-10
12-14	Spatial Orientation	12-14
6-8	Synchronization of Movement	6-8

(Grasso)

Athlete development is not a matter of luck or chance; however, a lack of guidance, education and understanding impedes true athletic and basketball development in the United States. "The assumption here [United States] is that if a large, healthy population base is available, then a process based on competition and letting the strong survive allows the best athletes to surface. This system has traditionally worked well for the US. However, as other nations take a more systematic approach to the nurturing of young athletes, we may fall behind," (Gambetta, 2002).

The LTAD model offers some guidance to balance youth athletic development. At eleven years old, for instance, a 70:30 training to competition ratio is recommended. Therefore, winning and competing is not the end-goal; winning a fifth grade championship is not as important as continued development of motor skills. "If fundamental motor skill training is not developed between the ages of eight to eleven and nine to twelve respectively for females and males, a significant window of opportunity has been lost, compromising the ability of the young player/athlete to reach his/her full potential," (Balyi and Hamilton, 2003). Given the physical education cuts plaguing school systems, teams, leagues and coaches need to include more players and train their fundamental motor skills, rather than cutting athletes. Even if these young athletes never play competitive athletics after elementary or middle school, the motor skill development aids their recreational activities throughout life; a child who quits playing sports or who is cut before developing these motor skills is less likely to pursue recreational activities during his life because he is not as adept and takes longer to learn and master new sports-specific skills. The LTAD model is not just a guiding principle for future professional athletes; it benefits all athletes, regardless of potential.

Why use a Long Term Athlete Development Model?

Children progress through different stages as they develop; the LTAD model reconciles athletic development with natural development. "From early childhood to maturation, people go through several stages of development, which include pre-puberty, puberty, post-puberty and maturation. For each development stage there is a corresponding phase of athletic training: Initiation (pre-puberty), Athletic Formation (puberty), Specialization (post-puberty), and High Performance (maturation)," (Bompa). Sports scientists and other nations use these principles to take a proactive approach to athlete development. These models provide a guide for athletes, coaches and league organizers to follow to insure each athlete receives the best opportunity to reach his peak performance, which should be the end-goal of all parents, administrators and coaches.

When I was in 5th or 6th grade, I won a local math contest. Suddenly, everyone viewed me as the smartest in my class and my dad envisioned a well-paid career as an engineer. However, despite my mathematical promise, I remained in all my classes, receiving a well-rounded education. When I reached college, I chose my major and specialized; I picked English, though my very first professor said I did not write well enough to be an English major. I never took a college math class and make a living writing and coaching basketball, not as an engineer.

In the sports world, parents and coaches encourage athletes to specialize in one sport at an early age because they believe one needs an advantage against the competition. In athletics, we choose specialization instead of well-rounded.

When I reached calculus, I realized I was an average math student; I excelled at one area of math: logic word problems. Imagine if I had specialized in math throughout high school only to discover I was fairly average and had developed no other subjects or skills. My struggles would extend far beyond school. Fortunately, I studied all subjects in high school.

If players specialize in sports too early, they run a similar risk. If a child chooses basketball because he is a precocious shooter at eleven years old, only to realize in high school he is not a power/anaerobic athlete, his basketball career ends and his alternatives are limited due to his lack of well-rounded motor skill development. Development deficiencies limit his effectiveness on the court and curtail opportunities in other activities as well.

The LTAD model parallels the school environment and encourages young athletes to develop a wide range of skills early and specialize late, after building a foundation of general motor skills. Schools have guidelines which measure each student and tell parents and teachers whether the student has the requisite skills to perform at the next grade level. Currently, no guidelines exist beyond the indiscriminant opinion of a particular coach. The LTAD provides guidelines to insure each child develops in an age-appropriate manner.

When a young athlete first plays basketball, coaches ignore movement skills, though they are the basis for basketball. In math, young students start with simple problems and progress annually to tougher and tougher levels; however, at each level of math, one needs the skills learned in the early grades. In basketball, no such gradual progression exists; a nine year old plays essentially the same game as a high school senior and oftentimes with a very similar training schedule. Basic addition and subtraction is not interchangeable with calculus, so why do we view youth and high school basketball as one? A child is not a small adult.

The LTAD creates a gradual progression whereby coaches teach athletes to play the game in stages, rather than all at once. With an expectation to win, a youth coach has little time to teach the basics and prepare his team for a game; so, with the "Peak by Friday" mentality, he prepares his team for the game to the detriment of his players' development. At the very beginning, actual basketball skills comprise very little of the practice time, as players learn to move without a ball before the ball and competition is added: one adds and subtracts before doing long division and athletes need to move well before dribbling and playing defense.

Unfortunately, parents, administrators and players fail to recognize the value in baby steps and gradual progression, which is why scientific evidence and the LTAD model are important tools. Research concludes that too much competition stunts an athlete's development.

In New Zealand, all athletes between 9-14 years, regardless of sport, participate in the same training as part of the Long Term Athletic Development System of New Zealand. The following list shows the New Zealand's LTAD basic curriculum:

Day One: Aquatics (stroke technique, conditioning)
Day Two: Ball Skills (hand-eye, foot-eye and dexterity development)
Day Three: Gymnastics (spatial awareness, systematic strength, dynamic balance, torso strength)
Day Four: Strength Training (skill acquisition, system strength, torso strength)

(Grasso, Vol. 80)

Imagine a youth basketball coach spending an entire practice on gymnastics, rather than ball skills. But, are spatial awareness, systematic strength, dynamic balance and torso strength important to basketball? Is there transfer between the fundamental motor skills learned in one activity and another activity? These skills are imperative for basketball success, yet a revolt would occur if a coach used gymnastics to train basketball players for one of his practices. Parents prefer their son or daughter learn another half dozen out of bounds plays than practice something with no visible relevance to basketball.

Sports scientists understand there is a better way to train athletes, whether recreational or elite, and the LTAD is a model for this enhanced, balanced training. The LTAD rationalizes athletic development and emphasizes the needs of the athlete, not the coach, parents or administrators. Basketball Canada recently implemented a seven stage model in its efforts to organize youth basketball development.

Basketball Canada's Development Model

Stage 1 – FUNdamentals: 5 – 7 years of age (community programs)
Stage 2 – Games approach: 8-9 years of age (community programs)
Stage 3 – Skills/Mini basketball [first exposure to 5 on 5]: 10-12 years of age (clubs/community)
Stage 4 – Train to Train: 13- 15 years of age (Schools, clubs, Centers for Performance)
Stage 5 – Train to Compete: 16-18 years of age (schools, clubs, Center for Performance)
Stage 6 – Learn to Win: 18 – 21 years of age (University, National Teams)
Stage 7 – Train to Win: National Teams

"We want to develop 'global players'. This means every player develops every skill. We encourage this through 15-16 years old. After this it is recommended to train players in all skills, but in competition we know coaches will begin to specialize. We are trying to discourage coaches from constantly selecting the early maturing athlete," says Mike MacKay, Canada's Manager of Coach Education and Development.

Canada's model features a basketball development pyramid; at the bottom of the pyramid is Fundamentals: movement/basketball (A fundamental is the how and why of a skill. How do you shoot and why do you shoot?); next is technical skills (A technical skill is the when of a skill. When do I shoot? It involves decision making); then strategies (A strategy is the long term plan for organizing the players. My strategy for ½ court defense is to force sideline) and finally tactics (A tactic is a short term adjustment to the strategy for a specific game. For this team we will trap the ball in the corner).

Fundamentals account for the largest time allotment; many American teams spend the most time on strategies and tactics with basic fundamentals receiving little time or emphasis. "Players do not reach their full potential because they are too early on sacrificed for the result. Their development is stagnated for the principle 'the result takes precedent over how it is achieved,'" (Michels). The following five stage model aims to correct the current flaws in the American system and emphasize the individual's development at younger ages, while harnessing the same competitiveness which makes American players great.

By following the LTAD model, recreational athletes learn more skills and have more fun, while elite athletes develop a greater base of skills to enhance their play as they reach adult basketball. Athletes do not develop overnight or by accident. The LTAD provides a model to guide athletes from pre-puberty through adult basketball in a sensible, efficient manner.

Chapter 5:
Introduction to the Five Stage Model

The United States basketball model features five stages: (1) Foundation; (2) Fundamentals; (3) Training; (4) Competition; and (5) Performance. However, this book details stages 1-4, which comprise youth development; the fifth stage covers adult basketball, whether competitive (college or professional) or recreational.

In past generations, teams developed in the winter and players developed in the summer; multilateral skills developed naturally through playing multiple sports and engaging in an active childhood. Early specialization, overuse injuries and year-round club basketball did not exist; consequently, a plan for year-round development or an organization to oversee basketball development was unwarranted.

However, youth sports is now a billion dollar industry supporting personal trainers, private workout facilities, year-round youth basketball leagues and teams, exposure events and more. Athletes play only one sport and train competitively before they are potty-trained. Due to these changes, more planning and organization is needed to nurture the talents of recreational and elite players.

Other nations' sports federations organize long term athlete development to maximize the potential of all its athletes. Professionalizing the youth development system serves the athletes' best interests, while the United States' amateur system exploits athletes and parents. The professional system uses science to guide athlete development, while competing interests pull American children in different directions with little thought to the child's feelings or future.

The Spanish Federation's Youth Basketball Program utilizes Player Development Centers for players ages 14-18. The Spanish system starts with summer camps for 10-14 year olds where coaches teach and evaluate potential prospects that they follow through the year. Select individuals join the Player Development Centers where "the goal is to help basketball players between 14 and 18 years of age train in the most efficient way so basketball is compatible with their studies and personal development," (Sergio).

The Centers emphasize "long-term training," which is absent in the United States. "Too many youth coaches think their own success with the team is very important. This is at the expense of the unconstrained development of the youth players," (Michels). In this results-driven system, young athletes train like mini-professionals, not children, and "adult training programs are superimposed on young athletes. This is detrimental because it means that coaching is conducted without regard for the principles of childhood development," (Balyi). Simply put, a child is not just a small adult; a child experiences different stages of physical and psychological development which cannot be rushed or ignored.

There are four major components of basketball: athletic, psychological, tactical and technical. Psychological skills are intertwined within each of the other skills; tactical, technical and athletic skills develop interdependently, as each skill requires and complements the other skills. While examined in isolation, tactical skills are pointless without technical shooting ability; technical shooting ability is useless without athleticism to defend; and athletic skills are wasted without game awareness.

Athletic skills are the general motor skills, the ABC'S of athleticism (Agility, Balance, Coordination and Speed) and five bio motor qualities: speed, strength, endurance, flexibility and coordination. Basketball requires a strong foundation of these skills, as increased athleticism enhances one's ability to execute basketball skills like shooting, ball handling, cutting and playing defense.

Tactical skills are the game's foundation; without tactical skills, basketball is HORSE. In the vernacular, tactical skills are the games X's and O's. Tactical skills are game skills: movement without the ball, setting and using screens, passing to the open teammate, defensive rotations, etc. Players with advanced tactical skills have a "feel" for the game or good court awareness. They have a high basketball I.Q. In many ways, this "feel" makes good players great and the great players almost unstoppable.

While technical skills and tactical skills work simultaneously, technical skills are the basketball-specific skills most readily associated with the game: shooting, ball handling, passing, etc. These skills are most easily drilled and instructed in isolation, though their worth is measured in concert with tactical skills.

In past generations, American players were known for their feel, the smoothness and creativity of their game borne through their development in unstructured environments. Nearly every great American player played pick-up games on the playground as an instrumental part of their development. American players now develop solely in structured systems. Coaches run structured systems and competitive basketball runs year-round, leaving little time for players to work on their own game or to play pick-up games at the park. Many coaches fault pick-up games for players' bad habits; however, informal play is the best environment for development and learning.

Renowned Dutch soccer coach Rinus Michels writes:

"My position is: street soccer is the most natural educational system that can be found…it is always the competitive form, where youth players learn from their mistakes, unconscious of the technical, tactical, mental and physical qualities they are developing through the scrimmages being played…In African and South American countries, where the conditions for street soccer are favorable, you can immediately notice that youth players have a head start. They go through a more varied technical and tactical development within their own experiences. Therefore, the 'feeling' for the game is better," (Michels).

Substitute the United States for Africa and South America and basketball for soccer and the same statement bears truth.

Informal games-whether pick-up games at the park, at recess or open gyms-provide players a competitive environment without pressure to perform. In this environment, players train skills and develop the feel for the game. When one plays games every day, he learns to move, to set picks, to get open, to make shots; he enters formal basketball with a varied skill set. When I was in 5th-8th grade, we played every day at recess. Our games were competitive, yet there was no fear of failure or making a mistake; if someone tried an around the back pass, no coach benched him. Our school team was successful, but much of our success was due to our informal playground games. In formal games, we had our system, but also a good feel for the game. Today, due to safety issues, less recess time, more homework, more extracurricular activities and responsibilities, more video games, etc. players do not play as much informal basketball and it negatively impacts players' development.

In the Dutch soccer federation in 1985, Michels and the other national team coaches met to devise an organized plan to improve Dutch soccer; part of the plan was a commitment to street soccer. The answer, since street soccer had been replaced by soccer academies was to use informal scrimmages in every academy training session. In today's basketball system, devote more time toward play. At the youngest ages, devote almost the entire training session toward play in some form, not separate units for technical drills and tactical drills. Players learn the game best through playing the game.

Too much coaching can backfire. According to the *Journal of Experimental Psychology: Applied,* athletes who learn the intricacies of a game on their own perform better than those who are heavily coached. British researchers split 26 junior tennis players into three groups, two of which were told to figure out a skill without instruction. The third group, which was explicitly coached, learned quickly but overthought each move, says study author Mark Williams, PhD of the Research Institute for Sport and Exercise Sciences. In coaching a child, 'encourage him to solve problems, as opposed to providing all the answers,' says Williams, (*Men's Health*, November 2005).

In an educational sense, active learners learn better than passive learners; that is, students involved in the learning process are more motivated to learn than students who simply follow the teachers orders. When working as a T.A. for Education 180 at UCLA, we learned to faciliate the discussion and lead students through probitive questioning, but not to give students all the answers. Educate derives from the Latin roots which mean "to lead out;" to educate is not to fill up a student with knowledge, but to guide the student to an awareness and understanding. Learning on the basketball court differs little from classroom learning; athletes learn best when they are motivated, interested and involved in the learning process. When all learning is coach-driven, athletes lose motivation and interest and learning suffers; players become robotic on the court, simply following orders while on auto-pilot, no longer thinking or feeling the game.

At the Spanish Player Development Centers, "players are taught simple movements and situations and then move up to situations that are more complex," (Sergio). At the Center, "we think this part of the program [small-sided games working on collective fundamentals] is an essential step that allows the player to learn how to play together with his teammates and develop his strategic intelligence," (Sergio). In education parlance, this is the whole-part-whole teaching method; start with the game (the whole); teach simple movements and play small-sided games (part) and then return to the full game with improved skills and understanding (whole).

By empowering athletes to take charge of the game, playing a less structured, more free-flowing style, athletes are motivated to learn and develop. Coaches guide the process, giving players tools to compete and organize their play, but athletes drive the action in the game. Overcoaching inhibits the learning process and creates a coach-centered environment.

The tactical skill development goal is to nurture and foster the feel for the game in all players in an effort to improve individual's decision-making abilities and court awareness. Through more game play at a young age, athletes enjoy the experience, learn the game and are motivated to improve and play more basketball. As athletes age, coaches organize these skills and enhance their development. At the highest levels, coaches develop systems around the players' skill sets and insure players develop a feel for playing with their teammates in a style which uses the team's strengths. Through the development process, remain athlete-centered and empower athletes to use their skills.

The athletic skill training goal is injury prevention and performance enhancement. Basketball is a game of quick, powerful movements requiring agility and explosiveness. Basketball players exhibit unparalleled athleticism and coordination, combining prodigious athletic feats like forty inch vertical jumps with ball skills, balance and hand-eye coordination to complete a basketball-specific skill.

During Stages 1 and 2, athletes learn and train a wide variety of skills (loco motor, non-loco motor and manipulative); this multi-lateral development provides a strong athletic foundation. Stage 3 transitions athletes from the learning stages to the competitive stages through increased emphasis on training load and intensity. In Stage 4, training specificity, testing and performance training increase.

Basketball is a simple game; the following four stage progression gradually builds upon simple concepts, teaching players how to play the game and progressing from simple to more complex and general to specific. The first stage takes a skill like movement without the ball and introduces a simple concept: get open; very little technical knowledge or explanation is needed. In the second stage, the basic instruction of "get open" grows more specific, as players get open in areas where they can attack the basket or present a passing lane to a teammate. In the third stage, the basic concept gets more specific, as players concentrate on using screens to get open. In the final stage, coaches take the basics and build an appropriate system for his personnel, so each player gets open in specific spots using specific cuts or screens. Unfortunately, the current learning paradigm skips the first three stages and moves players directly to the complex and specific. Use this model to guide basketball development over a period of years, not a matter of days.

Chapter 6:
The Foundation Stage

The Foundation Stage
Age: 8-10 years
Objective: Introduce basketball through fun, active training and develop general movement skills essential to basketball success.

Stage one introduces the young athlete to basketball's basic rules and strategy. Playing the game builds interest, but full 5v5 games lack action, as each possession involves few players. Players lack spatial awareness and cognitive skills required to play basketball, so games denigrate into bumblebee ball.

Basketball is a game of movement and players need general movement skills. Basketball coaches coach basketball; few coaches teach general motor skills. Just as an aspiring writer masters his ABC's before he writes a novel, an athlete must develop the ABC's of athleticism: Agility, Balance, Coordination and Speed. Skipping the basics inhibits players' mastery of more complex skills. If an athlete cannot run and stop on balance, how can he shoot the ball? Balance precedes every other aspect of shooting (NBA players have remarkable balance, even when it appears they are off-balance).

Training must be fun, active and promote learning; nothing drives a child away from a sport faster than boring practices consisting of drill after drill with no apparent connection to the game. Drills have its place, and young athletes need improvement, but training can be fun and encourage learning and development. "The object is to remove the idea that play must become work if children are to improve, so challenges replace technique practices, and drills make way for carefully structured games," (Launder).

No child signs up for a sports league to win. Winning becomes important because adults emphasize winning and kids follow their cues. "What seems to be missing in North American youth sport is the whole concept of activity without immediate purpose," (Grasso). Emphasize learning and fun, not competition and winning. This is a preparation stage, the first step toward a life of sports activities, not a season-long quest for a championship. "If the children later decide to leave the competitive stream, the skills they have acquired during the [Foundation] phase will still benefit them when they engage in recreational activities, which will enhance their quality of life and health," (Balyi and Hamilton, 2003). And, if the child remains in the competitive stream, the increased athleticism provides a better foundation.

Athletic Skills

Athletic Skills Training Goal: Speed, coordination, execution of proper movement patterns, fundamentals of movements, exposure to multiple skills.
Emphasis: Fun and games to develop skills and athleticism.

Stage 1 represents a pivotal age for youth athletic development; in many ways, this stage determines the athlete's ultimate success more than any other stage. Expose athletes to a multitude of general skills; devote more time to athletic skills training than tactical or technical training to prepare players for long term development and success.

Utilize scientific principles in training; skill development should be fun, not too technical, but coaches must understand the basic science behind the training to elicit the best results.

Through the four stage model, athletes move from general skills to specific skills and simple movements to complex movements; sports skills combine multiple general skills. Before athletes exhibit the grace, balance and agility of an NBA superstar, they master the basic fundamental components, the ABC's of athleticism, and train the five bio motor qualities (Speed, Strength, Flexibility, Endurance and Coordination).

Stage 1 introduces and teaches general movement skills and patterns to young athletes; these movements form the foundation of all athletic actions. The general movement skills trained include loco motor skills (running, skipping, jumping, bounding, etc.); non-loco motor skills (twisting, turning, balancing, etc.); and manipulative skills (throwing, kicking, catching, trapping, striking). Once the athletes understand proper execution of these skills, use a Dynamic Warm-up (See *Appendix*) at the beginning of each practice to train and refine these skills. The dynamic warm-up is neuromuscular training; it trains the proper neuromuscular patterns for movement. As the neuromuscular system improves its efficiency, athletes move more quickly and explosively.

Movement Skills: Loco motor, Non-Loco motor and Manipulative

Informal play during a practice session nurtures the natural learning process. Youth sports suffer from the extremes: coaches either instruct too little or too much; they either allow players to scrimmage the entire practice or teach every nuance. Optimal learning occurs during the activity; some instruction is necessary, but, error toward too little coaching, as opposed to too much coaching.

Emphasize proper techniques. The natural progression from march to skip to run, the proper squat pattern, and the proper lateral push teach skills incorporated in basketball skills. Too many coaches teach an athletic skill and a basketball skill simultaneously; before teaching a player to shoot, teach the player to bend properly by pushing his hips back and sitting down through his heels. A player who cannot bend properly to maintain balance and generate power from his lower body will have flawed upper body mechanics; rather than teaching lower body and upper body mechanics simultaneously, instruct a proper squat first and re-emphasize the movement later when introducing shooting technique. Leaning to squat properly during the Dynamic Warm-up facilitates basketball skill execution.

ABC'S

This stage features the first critical period for speed development. "Linear, lateral and multi-directional speed should be developed and the duration of the repetitions should be less than 5 seconds. This is often called the 'agility, quickness and change of direction window.' Again, fun games should be used for speed training and the volume of the training should be lower," (Hamilton and Balyi, 2003). Most sports require quick bursts of speed and athletes rarely reach maximum velocity. Use drills like *Tennis Ball Drop, Red Light-Green Light* and *Get-up Tag* to train acceleration. Incorporate these drills at the end of the warm-up. While this limits time spent with the ball, enhanced athleticism improves the players' basketball-specific skill.

A simple drill like *Tennis Ball Drop* has several important components. First, the drill teaches acceleration, as the athlete sprints five to ten feet to catch the tennis ball. Second, the drill trains reaction time and visual awareness, the reaction to a visual cue (the dropped ball). Third, the drill enhances hand-eye coordination, as the athlete catches the ball, and directional awareness, as the athlete anticipates its flight and speed. To train dexterity, force players to catch the ball with their weak hand. Of course, a child has no idea he is developing multiple skills, as his one concern is catching the ball and staying in the game.

Basketball is a game of quick movement; prospective basketball players should concentrate on training for speed and quickness; even if the players leave basketball for another sport, these attributes form the basis of most team sports.

Tactical Skills

Goals: Getting open, passing under pressure, basic man principles, squaring to an operational position.
Emphasis: Introduce basic basketball concepts through small-sided games.

During Stage 1, amend the rules and play small-sided games to create an environment for fun, learning and development through play. At its most basic, eliminating the technical skill components from basketball leaves keep away. Keep away requires players to get open and pass and receive the ball under duress. In the beginning of Stage 1, getting open and passing under pressure (keep away) are the most important skills to develop; however, rather than just playing games of keep away, incorporate basketball violations like traveling. *Volleyball Passing* teaches players to be strong with the ball, to pivot to find open teammates, to pass under pressure and to make cuts to get open within a confined space. *Americanized Net Ball* stresses the same elements in a greater area and incorporates shooting and scoring. Similarly, *3v3 Football* is a passing and getting open game, while *3v3/No Dribble* adds shooting and scoring.

These games require some basic instruction; introduce basic passes, pivots and other concepts from the Technical Skills section. However, once in the modified game, allow athletes to make decisions and plays. Rather than practicing skills in isolation, prepare players for formal competition through modified and small-sided games because decision-making skills and ability to handle defensive pressure are the biggest precursors to success, especially at this age.

These games incorporate and emphasize skill development in a basketball-like environment. Lessons do not transfer from drills to games at this age, so the game-like atmosphere is more conducive to player development. Drills fail to replicate the game environment, and the lessons from the drill are not applicable when the player is presented with a game atmosphere or challenge. While radically altering the game, ANB eliminates the greatest problem with youth basketball: jump balls, while enabling the ball handler to find an open teammate or shoot rather than fight a defender. Also, ANB encourages shots from closer to the basket, and, by eliminating the dribble, defensive instruction focuses on the man, not help side position, which is a hard concept for young athletes.

Americanized Net Ball runs counter to the "Peak by Friday" crowd of overzealous parents and overly competitive coaches. However, it builds good habits that translate to future success. Additionally, players are engaged and learn new skills in a fun, competitive environment, rather than running purposeless drills that lack meaning. "Children thrive on challenges. Children are always in search of opportunities to gain skills and prove themselves," (Damon). ANB provides the challenge and the opportunity to prove oneself, and a real game opportunity to learn and master new skills, an opportunity lost in typical youth league practices and games.

Small-sided games create a competitive learning environment where each player is involved more actively: the perfect teaching tool for younger athletes. "What a player does in a game is almost always influenced in some way by an opponent, who is not always predictable. This means that when youngsters try to apply what they have practiced in a drill to the scramble of a game, both technique and skill often breakdown because players cannot anticipate the defender's reactions," (Launder). 2v2 is ideal because players practice individual skills with plenty of space to maneuver; they also incorporate team elements like finding a teammate who has a better shot, getting open and playing help defense. "The basic rule is…beginners need plenty of space to play effectively," (Launder).

Two-on-two provides an optimal environment to introduce basic tactical skills like the give-and-go (basketball's most basic and fundamental tactical skill) and the screen-and-roll. The screen-and-roll is the easiest screen scenario to teach because an on-ball defender is always in the same space: defending the ball. This eliminates the ambiguities of the off-ball screen.

Small-sided games offer more space to offensive players to hone their technical skills. Full games at a young age favor the bigger, stronger players who dominate defensively and go coast to coast for lay-ups. While exciting for the player and his parents, this scenario does little to develop players. Small-sided games maintain more equitable competition, as finding four similarly skilled players is easier than finding ten. Technical offensive skills like passing, seeing the floor, shooting and dribbling develop slowly and small-sided games offer more repetitions and fewer stoppages. These games force defensive players to cover more ground, stay in front of a ball handler without reaching or fouling and help and recover; in a 5v5 game, off-ball defenders are uninvolved or flock to the ball, creating bumblebee ball. Small-sided games insure more action, which equates to more fun for young athletes learning skills.

Currently, the top 2-3 players develop because they dominate the ball, and the gap between these top players and everyone else widens; many others quit from boredom and frustration. The lack of action decreases their motivation to play and they leave the game, and possibly all organized sports, for another activity.

Technical Skills

Technical Skills Training Goal: Teach basics (stopping, starting and pivoting), lay-ups, ball handling, and passing.
Emphasis: Fun, teaching skills to enable small-sided competition and modified rules games.

Emphasize game play and athletic skill development; however, technical skill development is necessary for players to play modified rules or small-sided games. Seasons and practices are short, so coaches cannot possibly teach everything; emphasize lay-ups and the basics to prevent unnecessary turnovers (jump balls and travels at this age). While winning games is unimportant, practice must enhance players' ability to compete.

Teach basic concepts; specifically, teach players to stop on-balance (stride-stop and quick stop); to pivot (front and reverse); and to protect the ball (operational, diamond the ball, space step). These skills provide the foundation and eliminate the most frequent violations. Developing good footwork now improves one's ability to acquire new and more advanced skills later.

Use *Utah Line Drills* as an extension of the *Dynamic Warm-up* to teach these skills at the beginning of each practice:

- **Quick Stop**: A quick stop (commonly called a jump stop) is a two-footed stop on a one-count, either when receiving a pass or off the dribble, with feet wider than shoulder width, knees bent and butt down to stop under control.
- **Stride Stop**: A quick 1-2 (step-step) stop, off the catch or the dribble. The first step becomes the pivot foot.
- **Pivot Foot**: When stopped, the player can move one foot, as long as the other foot stays on the ground (the pivot foot). Players make a front pivot (pivoting in the direction the player is facing) or reverse pivot (pivoting opposite the direction player is facing) depending on the situation and defense.
- **Operational**: Similar to the triple threat concept, as the player is a threat to shoot, pass or drive. Position the ball in the shooting pocket; protect the ball with quick fakes, pivots or by ripping the ball through while maintaining an attacking position with shoulders squared to the basket.
- **Space Step**: Diamond the ball and step foot between the defender's legs to force defender to take a step backwards (If defender doesn't move, rip through and go past him). Protect ball with the head and elbow. Use to create space for a shot, pass or an offensive move.
- **Diamond the Ball**: When protecting the ball, put it by the back ear, with elbows out, forming a small diamond shape. This achieves the same goal as "chinning the basketball," but is more practical.

These six concepts enable young players to play without constant stoppages for traveling violations and jump balls. Players who are strong with the ball, rather than turning away from the defense and "turtling," have a head start moving forward; even high school players do not always catch and pivot aggressively. Squaring to the basket in an operational position is a skill not to overlook, as every offensive play requires players to receive a pass and square to the basket for a shot, drive or pass; this is the most basic skill, but the most important, as things fall apart without a strong foundation.

Teach players to shoot lay-ups with both hands. When I was in elementary/middle school, our team was very successful, winning two Parochial League Championships; one reason, I believe, is my father/coach's insistence on making us use both hands. We made twenty lay-ups in a row on both sides to start each practice. I imagine we had practices where we shot lay-ups for half the practice, but by season's end, twenty lay-ups in a row was a short warm-up. Also, the practice requirement encouraged anyone who was not confident in his weak hand to practice on his own.

Many lay-up varieties exist; however, when teaching the lay-up, start with the hand behind the ball. Aim for the near top corner of the square on the backboard. Hit the backboard on the way down for a softer shot. Protect the ball from the defense; many players rock the cradle- a rocking motion with the ball. This rocking motion gives the defense a chance to strip the ball or disrupt the shot.

Initially, isolate new skills. Therefore, start a lay-up drill without a dribble or approach. Start just beyond the block facing the basket with feet together. For a right-handed lay-up, step and jump off the left foot; rotate the ball into shooting position and shoot a right-handed lay-up.

Next, take a big step away from the basket and practice with two steps and a dribble at walking speed. The proper form, not speed, is most important. Start with feet together; step with right foot and dribble. Step with left foot, pick-up the dribble, jump and shoot the lay-up.

Finally, move to the elbow area and work on a full speed, one dribble lay-up. Use three steps; for a right-handed lay-up, step with the left foot and dribble. Step with the right foot, pick up the dribble, step with the left foot, jump and shoot the lay-up. Stride to cover ground; eliminate the baby steps and stutter-steps players commonly use.

Use the *Extension Lay-up Drill*, *X-Lay-ups*, *Full Court Lay-ups* and other drills to practice shooting lay-ups at game speed from different angles; shooting shots similar to those one shoots in the game is the best practice. After mastering the basic technique, increase the speed of execution.

Incorporate ball handling training into the *Utah Line Drills* and lay-up drills. Teach the basic dribbling technique: dribble the ball with fingers and calluses, not the palm. Use an appropriately sized ball for young players to develop control.

The two basic dribbles at this age are the protect dribble and the speed dribble. Incorporate instruction into a basic game like *Red Light-Green Light*. On a green light, use the speed dribble: push the ball forward and dribble around waist height; cover as much distance per dribble as possible. On a red light, stop in a protect dribble: use a wide stance; dribble the ball straight down by the back foot; use an arm bar with the off hand to protect from the defensive player. In addition to the traditional verbal cues of red and green light, modify the game to train visual cues and insure players dribble with head up the floor. Give players directions that correspond to visual cues; a palm up equals a red light, etc.

Introduce players to basic passes, but use other drills to teach passing basics. The execution of basic passes is not typically the problem; players need practice passing under pressure and/or to a moving target. Basic games covered in the tactical section effectively train passing skills.

Basketball Passes

- **Chest Pass**: Elbows out, hands on the side of the ball, extend straight from one's chest, aiming for teammates chest and finish with thumbs down, chest over thigh.
- **Bounce Pass**: Similar to a chest pass, but bounce the ball half to two-thirds of the way to teammate. The ball should bounce up to the player's thigh.
- **Overhead Pass**: Pass from the forehead, not behind one's head. Aim for teammate's throat. Follow-thru and finish with thumbs down. Used most frequently as an outlet pass or a skip pass.

- **Wrap around Pass** (Air and bounce pass): Extend around defense with hands and feet. Step to the side of defense and use two hands on ball; follow through with outside hand. Use as a post entry pass.
- **Hook Pass**: Pass off the dribble. Hook the ball over head and follow through. Use on a pick and roll.
- **Push Pass** (air or bounce pass): Pass off a dribble. One hand behind the ball pushes the ball. Most commonly used pass, as it protects the ball from the defense by using the outside hand to throw the pass. Quickest pass off the dribble.
- **Baseball Pass**: One-hand overhead pass like a baseball player. Finish with thumbs down to control the pass.

Beginners need more playing and less drilling. Therefore, technical instruction is de-emphasized in Stage 1. Coaches prioritize skills and maximize practice time to insure development, but also enthusiasm. Practice is not work, and players do not have to forfeit fun to improve. Players need basic instruction, especially with lay-ups, but devote most of practice to small-sided games where there is space and opportunity for a young athlete to dribble, pass and shoot. More specific and intense technical instruction and training occurs in the following stages when athletes are equipped to use and develop their technical skills.

Stage 1 Drills

Athletic Skills

Tennis Ball Drop: Stand five feet away from an athlete and drop a tennis ball from shoulder height; as soon as the ball is dropped, the athlete accelerates and tries to catch the ball on its first bounce. Increase the distance as appropriate.

Get Up Tag: One player stands and the other player starts lying face down; when the coach says go, the first player starts running while the second player has to stand up, run and tag the first player within a certain distance (20 yards).

Tactical Skills

Americanized Net Ball: Played with two basic rule changes:

1. No dribbling. The ball must advance with a pass.
2. No blocking an offensive player's shot or stealing the ball from an offensive player. A defender may contest a shot or steal a pass, but it is a foul if the defender reaches or blocks, whether the reach or block is "all ball" or not.

Volleyball Passing: Two four-man teams play within the volleyball court lines between the 10-foot line and the end line. Teams must cut to get open and pivot to improve passing angles. Teams complete passes until one team reaches 100. On a turnover, the player committing the turnover must run out of bounds and do two push-ups, giving the new offensive team a brief man advantage. Counting is continuous, so teams pick up where they were when they last had the ball.

3v3 Football: Play 3v3 with no dribble. Objective is for one team to pass the ball the length of the floor and across the baseline (end zone). If a pass is intercepted, or if the ball goes out of bounds, the opponent attempts to pass the ball into its end zone.

3v3/No Dribble: Play 3v3 without the dribble. Objective is to pass, move and screen to get an open shot and make a basket. Depending on numbers, play to one basket (younger) or three baskets (older).

Technical Skills

Utah Line Drills: Players form five lines on the baseline and start in an operational position. On GO, the first five players jog to the free throw line, while the second five get in an operational position. Each group makes a quick stop at the free throw lines, half court and the baseline and waits for subsequent commands. The commands are: FRONT PIVOT, REVERSE PIVOT, JAB STEP, DRIVE STEP, RIP-THROUGH CROSSOVER STEP, SHOT FAKE or any combination.

Extension Lay-up Drills: Start on the wing at the three-point line, free throw line extended in an operational position. Spin the ball and receive on a one-count. Use one dribble; utilize a big first step and extend with the dribble.

- **Crossover step (right foot pivot) right hand lay-up**: Step to the basket with left foot. Dribble with the right, or outside, hand. Finish with a right-hand lay-up, jumping off the left foot.
- **Crossover step (right foot pivot) right hand reverse lay-up**: Same as above, except make a reverse lay-up with right hand on the left hand side of the basket.
- **Direct drive (left foot pivot) inside hand lay-up**: Step directly to the basket with right foot first. Push off with the left foot. Dribble with the right (outside) hand and finish with the left hand, jumping off the right foot.
- **Crossover step (left foot pivot) left hand finger roll**: Step with the right foot across the body to beat the defender to the middle. Dribble the ball with the left (outside) hand. Finish at the front of the rim with a finger roll.

X-Lay-ups: Player attempts to make as many lay-ups in thirty seconds (forty-five seconds, one minute) as possible. Player starts at the elbow, dribbles and attempts a lay-up. He must rebound the ball and then touch the baseline before running to touch the other elbow and returning for a lay-up from that side of the court. Continue in this pattern until time has elapsed.

Full Court Lay-ups: Players pair up and each pair has one ball. Drill begins with Player 1 sprinting up the wing and Player 2 passing the ball to P1. P1 receives the pass and attacks the basket for a lay-up. P2 becomes a defensive player and chases P1, attempting to prevent the lay-up. After shooting, P1 grabs the ball and steps out of bounds to outlet the ball to P2 and then becomes the defensive player. Next group starts when the first group gets to half court.

Red-Light-Green-Light: On a green light, take off with a speed dribble; on a red light, stop in a protect dribble. If the player fails to stop quickly or properly, he returns to the baseline. Winner is the first player to the other baseline.

Chapter 7:
The Fundamentals Stage

Age: 10-12
Objective: Continue general motor skill development; learn fundamental basketball-skills and progress to full court 5v5 games.
Training to Competition Ratio: 70:30

In Stage Two, emphasize basketball-specific skill training and expand general athletic skills. Basketball is a game of movement; practice movement skills-running, shuffling, jumping, landing, stopping-daily. Children need a wide range of abilities; an athlete who improves his hand-eye coordination, balance, spatial awareness and strength is better at every sport. "Adding a variety of athletic skill development into the programs of young (especially pre-adolescent) athletes serves to (a) broaden the youngsters' athletic ability through an enhanced nervous system (b) reduce the risk of potential injury by not making skill development one-dimensional (c) enhance their potential ability in any particular sport via developing global skill and (d) prevents against emotional burnout-which is a highly problematic issue in North American youth sports," (Grasso).

Balance technical and tactical training. During games, play to win; however, emphasize skill training, not game preparation, during practice. Coaches scream at players to bend their knees or move their feet quicker. However, one must instruct these skills and use drills to teach and build good habits. When a player makes a mistake, coaches quickly identify the basketball problem (missing short) and maybe even the general problem (poor balance), but miss the root (inability to squat). Each error is a symptom of poor general athletic skill development, which needs to be corrected before the player improves the sports-specific skill.

Individual development is essential. "During this time, children are developmentally ready to acquire general overall sports skills that are the cornerstones of all athletic development," (Balyi and Hamilton, 2003). Shooting is the most important skill; learning proper shooting technique with sufficient repetitions at this age builds the foundation for continued success. Many players develop bad habits because they shoot outside their range. Smart players learn proper form and shoot in their range. As confidence and strength build, extend range as a maker, not just a shooter. Those who shoot from too far away and develop bad habits may never reach their peak potential because of poor shooting habits; or, they require considerable time and effort re-learning proper shooting mechanics.

In this age, children are aware of winning and losing. For most, the final score is not the biggest issue; adults increase its importance. Players want to play and feel important; winning beats losing, but winning is not everything to young children. Competition is healthy, but the "will to win must come from within the child. Parents, activity leaders and trainers must only create conditions, through organizing matches and giving training sessions, in keeping with the perceived world of the child," (Michels).

Athletic Skills

Athletic Skills Training Goal: Coordination, sports skills, refinement of previously developed skills, additional exposure to various stimuli.
Emphasis: Adding stimuli to make games and drills more challenging.

In Stage 2, continue general athletic development, which complements general overall sports skills development. "This is the window of accelerated adaptation to motor coordination," (Balyi and Hamilton). This is a sensitive period for developing balance, movement adequacy, kinesthetic differentiation, reaction to acoustical and visual signals and rhythmic motion (Grasso).

General basketball practice and drills train the overall sports skills and motor coordination. Players manipulate a ball, whether shooting, passing, receiving or dribbling; train spatial awareness while judging distances between oneself and the offensive player he is defending; directional awareness when anticipating and chasing a rebound; visual awareness when sprinting down court and deciding whether to attack the basket or back out and set-up; temporal awareness in the shooting mechanics, especially at the free throw line and more. However, continued athletic development is necessary to enhance and refine skills.

Strength

Train general strength. General strength is body weight training: squats, lunges, push-ups, pull-ups, bar dips, etc. Also, train the core; the core encompasses the muscles that attach to the spine and pelvis. Core strength is the first step toward overall strength, as the core initiates movement and stabilizes the body when strengthening other areas. For instance, when doing a push-up, the athlete needs core strength to keep his body in a straight line and not allow his hips to sag or stick his butt in the air. Core strength, however, is more than training for a six pack; train all four muscles in the abdominal region (rectus abdominis, internal and external obliques and transverse abdominis) and the erector spinae (lower back). Use stability exercises, like the bridge and superman, and twists, like a medicine ball twist.

Movement Skills

Emphasize balance and coordination of movements. Using the same games as in Stage 1, add another element to increase the challenge and continue the body's adaptation to training. Train balance through *RLGL*; on the red light, players stop on one leg, rather than two. Combine *Get-up Tag* and *Tennis Ball Drop*, so the athlete lies prone and scrambles to his feet in an effort to catch the tennis ball. Play *Tag* while dribbling a basketball.

ABC'S

Two major components of agility are changing directions and lateral quickness. Basketball is a game with multiple direction changes, and players who change directions quickly and remain on-balance have the advantage against their opponents. Lateral quickness determines a player's defensive success, as defense is primarily played while moving laterally and backward.

Use a speed ladder to train agility and quickness. A speed ladder is a flat ladder used to train footwork and quickness. Dozens of patterns exist; be creative. Incorporate the speed ladder into stations at the beginning of practice or use as part of the warm-up or in conjunction with other skills.

An obstacle course is a fun way to train various skills; use a speed ladder, hurdles, cones, etc. Start by doing the "Icky Shuffle" through the speed ladder; sprint to half court and do a zigzag shuffle around cones to the baseline and do five push-ups; then, skip to half court and do twenty side-to-side hops; finally, pick-up a basketball and drive to the basket for a lay-up. This course incorporates an amazing array of skills and kids love the competition and challenge.

Other ideas for training agility and lateral quickness are the *T-Drill*, *Spoke Drill* and a Reaction Ball. Use the Reaction Ball instead of a tennis ball to add another element to the *Tennis Ball Drop Drill*. The Reaction Ball is a multi-sided ball that bounces in different, unpredictable directions.

Individual Defense

Individual on-ball defense is an athletic skill and an attitude. Teach lateral speed skills to improve individual defense. The defensive slide is taught as a slow, two step move where the athlete reaches with his first step and pulls his body under him. The more efficient technique is a push from the opposite leg (if going right, push away with the inside of the left leg). To cover more ground, especially when an offensive player has a step, use a crossover step; the general rule is never to cross one's feet, but watching the quickest NBA defensive players like Earl Boykins or Tony Parker dispels the theory.

To teach the defensive shuffle properly, start with one slide. To move to one's left, stand on the right foot with the left foot six inches off the ground. Push-off the right foot and move as far to the left as possible, staying low to the ground (not a hop) and landing in an athletic position with shoulders over knees, knees over toes and toes pointed straight ahead. As players learn the correct movement, add additional slides in a repetitive motion.

Progression

1) Individual Push
2) Multiple pushes in one direction
3) Three pushes and stop: Push three times and stop on one-foot, body in position to change directions. If pushing to the left push off the right foot and stop on the left foot with right foot six inches off the ground. Teach players to stop on-balance in a good athletic position; toes pointed forward with weight centered over the left leg or to the inside. Do not lean to the outside of the leg.
4) One change of direction: Three pushes in one direction and a quick change of direction; push to the starting point.
5) Lane-line Pushes: Work for thirty seconds doing defensive pushes from lane-line to lane-line; emphasize the quick change of direction and the push in the opposite direction.

To teach moving at a backward angle, as is most common when defending, teach a quick quarter turn and a crossover step. The quarter turn is a quick hop to turn the feet and hips slightly. Use the football drill where players face forward doing foot fire; on the whistle, players do a quarter turn and back and continue foot fire. Most defensive instruction teaches a plant and drop step; however, the more natural motion, and the motion of really quick players, is a quick hop to turn hips and feet. The hop moves the body in position to defend the change of direction move and keeps the body in an athletic position without any deviation (as between the foot and hip if doing a pivot and drop-step).

Next, use the crossover step because the offensive player gains a step on a change of direction move. A crossover step is quicker than a lateral shuffle because each step covers more ground; also, the crossover step keeps hips directed at the offensive player unlike a player who turns and sprints. A crossover step is like half-carioca: when moving to the left, the right foot crosses over in front of the left foot. As the right foot pushes down, the left foot steps and pushes. With these three techniques (the push, the quarter turn and the crossover step), players are prepared physically to play defense and their movement skills are more advanced than many high school and college players.

Finally, teach players to change directions on cuts. Most non-contact ACL injuries occur when the athlete cuts, plants or lands from a jump. General instruction is "plant and go," as part of a more involved drill. Instead, emphasize the proper body position: center of gravity and knee over foot. Use the step before the cut to lower the body's center of gravity. Show athletes exactly how to cut and practice the movement before incorporating other basketball skills. Use the *Ice Skater Drill* to teach the body position and lateral push and a *45-degree Bound* to teach a cutting movement. Incorporate change of direction training into the Utah Line Drills; emphasize straight, not curved lines. Do not rush fundamentals; take time to teach movements correctly.

Tactical Skills

Goals: Making cuts, setting and using an on-ball screen, help defense, basic team defense concepts.
Emphasis: Team basketball; Player and ball movement.

In the United States, Stage 2 begins competitive basketball, with national tournaments, bickering parents, all-star events, etc. However, Stage 2 is a vital development period and training and learning skills should remain the focus, not winning games or national championships. "In many countries, the development of the young players is inhibited. The players do not reach their full potential because they are too early on sacrificed for the result. Their development is stagnated for the principle 'the result takes precedent over how it is achieved,'" (Michels, 184).

Stage 2 emphasizes small-sided games, though teams compete in 5v5 games and tournaments. However, practice sessions, which ideally comprise about 75% of Stage 2 activities, center on small-sided play. When I played in Europe, our coach used small-sided, competitive games extensively. Small-sided games provide more repetitions; less wasted time, competitive situations, unpredictable environments, and contested shots. While drills have a place in teaching a new skill, drills cannot replicate game decision-making skills. Decision-making skills make or break the player, and players must learn to interpret and attack different situations. Unfortunately, coaches approach the learning environment in reverse, eliminating the decision-making process by running multiple drills where they are told what to do and what to expect and running set plays where they are told where to move and where to pass. Only at older ages do some coaches allow a certain measure of freedom, though players are ill-equipped because they never learned important game awareness skills. Even at the professional level, coaches control the action and eliminate free thinking.

Basketball is an unpredictable game; drills and set plays create a predictable sequence of events. Drills facilitate learning a new skill, but the competitive environment's unpredictability enhances skill mastery in a game context. I train players individually, teaching technical skills such as shooting and athletic skills like lateral movement. However, basketball is not played in isolation; players need repetition and instruction to take technical skills and apply them to a game atmosphere. Here is where small-sided games enhance individual instruction and transfer individual skills to the team game.

When learning to move without the ball, a drill cheats the offensive player, as the offensive player knows how he is to be defended. While sufficient for working on the technical skill of shooting off different cuts, this drill limits the offensive player's decision-making, which ultimately determines success in competition; if the offense never learns to read and react to defenders during training, he follows choreographed cuts during games, whether he moves to open spots or not. In some ways, drills and set plays eliminate common sense from athletes; a complete novice moves to an open spot because that makes sense; a player with decision-making skills moves to the open spot because it is the smart play; a well-drilled player follows directions, even if he is not open. Small-sided games eliminate the robotic, well-drilled player who cannot react to new situations during competition.

Building upon half court lessons, play *2v2 Rugby* to emphasize additional concepts in the full court. This game is especially effective if the team presses or plays against a press, which is the dominant form of youth games in California. The game creates a number of 1v0, 1v1 and 2v1 lay-up opportunities. Players train open court ball handling and ball handling versus back court defensive pressure. These three skills are important at this age in competitive basketball and provide a foundation for development. Mastering full speed lay-ups is an essential, but overlooked skill, and far more age-appropriate than the three-point shot.

To train half court skills, *3v3* is optimal. Most offensive sets or plays revolve around three players: passer, screener and cutter; the other two players space the floor. Even in most pick and roll situations, two players spread the defense and one off the ball player is positioned to shoot or make an easier pass to the roller, while the cutter (ball handler) uses the screen set by the screener.

In 3v3, players utilize all their skills in a competitive situation with space to take shots in their range. Defensively, players help and recover and defend on the ball, as no extra players exist to rotate into position or provide secondary help. 3v3 blends multiple players, allowing for advanced team tactical skill and decision-making skill development, while spreading the floor to give sufficient space. 3v3 trains the give and go cuts, screens away from the ball, screens on the ball, dribble penetration and kick, shooting, rebounding, passing, ball handling, etc.

As the player progresses through Stage 2, emphasize off-the-ball movement, spacing the floor away from dribble penetration, filling vacated gaps and setting and using screens. Again, while instruction is important to explain a player's options when receiving a screen, approaching the screen and exploiting the defense, emphasize the decision-making aspect in game context. Many players know in their mind when and what to do; however, when forced to read the defense and make a split-second decision, they fail. Experience playing and making decisions in an unpredictable environment, not more drills, will improve a player's analysis.

If these models are followed, players exit Stage 2 with decision-making skills required to play in a game, and a game awareness of how to use a screen, set a screen, handle ball pressure, pass and cut, find an open spot and more. Coupled with technical skill development, athletes are ready for more formal competition and a higher level of instruction as they enter Stage 3. Very few twelve year old players possess these skills today, as little emphasis is given to half-court play or off-ball movement; the emphasis is following directions, running to spots and choreographed presses and press breaks.

Technical Skills

Technical Skills Training Goal: Introduce basic skills, teach proper shooting mechanics, increase individual moves, practice basic defensive concepts.
Emphasis: Skill acquisition, general skill development, skill execution and playing against defenders.

Stage 2 training exposes players to a multitude of basketball-specific skills. Nobody masters these skills during this stage; physiologists and sports experts agree it takes ten years to master a skill at an elite level (Balyi). In this stage, emphasize the introduction and proper execution of the various basketball skills and encourage players to further practice these skills on their own.

Proper shooting form is the most essential skill. Shooting is the single most important technical skill in basketball and field goal shooting percentage is the number one determining factor in the outcome of games (Oliver).

Beyond shooting mechanics, expose players to additional ball handling moves, live ball moves, defense, passing and post play. Develop the basic coordination of movements: proper execution is more important than speed of execution. At the forthcoming levels, players master skills and train at optimal speeds. This stage merely begins the learning process which takes years to perfect.

I. Shooting Form

Teach players to be makers, not just shooters. After learning the proper shooting mechanics, encourage players to shoot inside their range: a player's range extends as far as he can shoot without a breakdown in form. Many players wildly shoot shots without any consideration of their range and saddle themselves with errors in their mechanics. The distance with which one can shoot is unimportant, and most players should shoot inside fifteen feet. The goal is to make shots, whether in a game or practice, and shooting from too far away only serves to make a player a worse shooter. It may hurt players' egos to spend time shooting close to the basket, but this training prepares players to progress in future stages, while players developing poor mechanics either stall their development as they age or must re-learn proper mechanics at some point in their future.

I use the BELIEF shooting method to teach players proper form and the *Three in a Row Drill* to restrict a player to his range. Belief is an appropriate acronym for shooting as confidence is the most important ingredient in shooting success. However, optimal biomechanical shooting mechanics exist:

Balance: Make sure players squat properly; many mistakes result from an improper bending movement. Shoot with shoulders over the knees and knees over the toes in an athletic position.

Eyes: Fine center on the basket. Choose a spot (front, back, middle), but be consistent every time.

Line (alignment): Straight line extends from the ball, through the hand, wrist, elbow, knee and foot.

Index Finger: Center index finger on the middle of the ball.

Extension: On the shot, the body extends from the ankles, knees and hips to supply the power for the ball. Elbow extends overhead, so the elbow is above the eyes at the finish.

Finish: Finally, wrist flexes to follow-through. Shoot all the way through the ball and keep fingers extended through the shot.

II. Live Ball Moves

Live ball moves incorporate the concepts outlined in Stage 1 with more fakes and additional moves. Live ball moves occur when the player has possession and use of his dribble. In these instances, the offensive player has his greatest advantage when he first receives the ball, as he is either open for a shot or receives the ball with his defender moving toward him, opposite the direction he wants to go; a quick move against the defender's momentum is better than a move against a defensive player who is set and ready to defend. The other important concept is: "A fake is not a fake if it looks like a fake," (Dave Hopla).

- **Drive Step**: A player's first step in an attacking drive. Attack the defensive player's top foot to force the defender to turn his hips. Use a big first step, with nose over toes. Attack directly past the defender; put shoulder on the defender's hip, going *body up, body in*. Knock away the defender's hand and keep the inside shoulder low. Extend with the dribble. Keep head and eyes up to see the floor.
- **Jab Step**: A small step used to set up a move, create space or keep the defender off balance. The jab step must be long enough to make the defender believe it is a drive step, but short enough to keep the offensive player well-balanced. Make a quick, hard step. Rip ball to knee. Keep 60-70% of one's weight on the pivot (push) foot to avoid the travel.
- **Shot Fake**: Utilize only the upper body; the lower body remains low and ready to explode. The eyes sell the fake and must look at the target. A good fake includes no wasted motion. Make an explosive fake to the hair line.
- **Pass Fake**: Use to move the defense or hold the help defense, similar to a quarterback faking a hand-off to hold the linebackers. As a rule, the pass fake is used to fake the player who is covering the pass receiver or to freeze scrambling defenders.
- **Ball Fake**: A smaller, quicker fake used against the player guarding the passer to create a passing angle. Fake low to make an air pass or fake high to throw a bounce pass. The pass follows directly from the fake with no wasted motion.

III. Ball Handling/Finishing

In Stage 2, players develop more ball handling moves and train by incorporating ball handling moves with shots around the basket. Players do not spend sufficient time making shots; in games, players lack the creativity necessary to take and make contested shots around the basket. In this stage, introduce reverse lay-ups, crossover lay-ups, up-and-under moves, running hooks and floaters from different angles.

Train different ball handling moves like a crossover, space dribble, hesitation dribble and fake crossover. Finish ball handling moves with a lay-up or shot; when I first coached in Europe, a coach told me the difference between American and European basketball was European drills always finished with a shot, while Americans did different drills for different skills. The emphasis in Europe was scoring or making the basket, which, the coach reasoned, is why European basketball is associated with better shooting and scoring than American basketball.

The *Number One Rule of Good Ball Handling* is to direct head and shoulders toward the offensive basket to enable vision of the entire court. When the defensive player directs the offensive player to the sideline or forces the offensive player into a protect dribble stance, the defensive player is winning the individual battle. These four moves enable an offensive player to control the defensive player, to attack the basket and to maneuver out of bad situations.

- **Crossover Dribble:** Use to change directions. Set-up the defender in one direction and execute a low crossover to go in the opposite direction.
- **Space Dribble**: Use to create space from the defensive player and square shoulders to the basket; essentially it is a backwards dribble in a protect dribble stance, using the width of the body to protect the ball. Push off on the inside foot and shuffle backward for one to two dribbles.
- **Hesitation Dribble:** A basic change of speed dribble used to keep the defense off-balance or set-up an attacking move.
- **Fake Crossover**: Use to move the defender in order to maintain a straight line drive. To execute the move, the hand makes a "C" on the downward flight of the dribble, bringing the ball to the middle of the body and then to the outside for the next dribble. To accentuate the ball fake, take a small jab step in the direction of the fake and lean the inside shoulder into the fake.

IV. Post Play

Post play instruction is important for all players because it incorporates many basic concepts which are applicable all over the court. While post players need a go-to move to each shoulder, and maybe a counter, the basics of post play are: reading the defense, using pump fakes and pivots and creating space for a shot or drawing a foul. Post play is using the body to create a shot rather than evading a defensive player. Use drills like the *Mikan Drill, Peth's Post Positioning Drill* and basic *Block2Block Post Move Drill* to teach basic footwork and finishing in the post and use 1v1 and 2v2 games to prepare players to use the moves in a game.

When a player understands how to use his body to create separation; to utilize pump fakes to keep the defender off-balance; and to use front and reverse pivots consecutively without traveling, he is a more well-rounded and effective player anywhere on the floor. Study the great scorers in recent NBA history and almost all players use fakes, pivots and spins much like a post player: MJ created space for a fade-away jump shot and then for his step-step counter move by getting into the defense and spinning away from the defender; Kobe does similar things; Paul Pierce uses spins, fakes and pivots to get himself to the foul line.

Stage 2 Drills

Athletic Skills

T-Drill: The athlete sprints ahead five feet, then backpedals to the beginning; he shuffles five feet to one side and back to the middle; shuffles to the other side and back to the middle.

Spoke Drill: Place one cone in the middle and eight cones around the perimeter. Athlete starts by sprinting forward and touching the first cone; he backpedals to the middle cone. Then, he moves at a 45-degree angle for the next cone; then laterally; then back at a 45-degree angle; then back pedals straight back and sprints forward. Each time, the athlete touches the middle cone before progressing to the next cone. This drill incorporates the crossover step, sprints, backpedals and shuffles.

Ladder Drills: Dozens of different patterns exist; a few examples:

Moving straight ahead: *one foot in; two feet in; shuffle* (start on the right side of the first square; left foot in, right foot in, left foot out; in next square, right foot in, left foot in, right foot out); *backward shuffle; in-out hops* (two feet in; two feet out); *one in-one out hops; 180-degree hops* (left foot starts in first square, right foot in second square; hop and land with right foot in second square and left foot in third square).

Moving laterally: *one foot in; carioca; scissor hops* (start with right foot in and left foot out; hop and land with left foot in and right foot out); *two feet in-two feet out.*

Ice Skater Drill: Stand on the right foot with left foot slightly behind the right foot, like an ice skater's stance. Push-off laterally, landing on the left foot on-balance. Push-off on the left foot and land on the right.

45-degree Bound: Like the ice skater drill, however, the athlete moves at a 45-degree angle forward. Athlete starts on his right foot and pushes laterally and forward, landing on his left foot.

Tactical Skills

2v2 Rugby is played best if there are 8 players; four teams of two players. Two teams play while two teams rest; players play 100% because a rest is up coming. A team remains on the court until scored against; if they score, they pick-up full court defense against a new team entering on offense. The "rugby" rule is only the dribble advances the ball in the backcourt; all passes must be backwards. This enables teams to work on the trap and recover defensively (the original reason I played the game) and teaches the offense proper spacing to receive a pass and advance quickly up court with the dribble.

3v3: Manipulate rules to teach different aspects of the game and keep games short (3-5 baskets). In the half court, call a violation any time a player passes and stands still, or catches and fails to square to the basket. Reinforce good habits and punish bad habits through the rules.

Technical Skills

Three in a Row: Player starts one foot from the front of the rim, directly in front of the basket. Using proper form, he shoots ball. Shooter makes three in a row and steps back. A miss means player takes one step forward. Work back to the free throw line.

Zone Shots: Player 1 shoots, Player 2 passes and Player 3 rebounds; use two balls. P1 shoots from the wing, while P2 throws skip passes from the opposite side; P3 rebounds and outlets to P2. P1 points inside foot to the rim and squares shoulders to the passer, hands up and knees bent. P1 receives pass, pivots to the basket and shoots. After shooting, he retraces his shot back to the starting point and waits for the next pass. Make ten and rotate.

Mikan Drill: Player makes a right hand lay-up. He grabs the rebound out of the net while stepping to the left side of the rim with his right foot. He jumps off the right foot and makes a left-hand crossover lay-up. Again, he rebounds the ball and steps with his left foot to the right side of the rim and makes a right hand lay-up. Keep the ball above the shoulders throughout the drill and complete without traveling. Shoulders should be square to the backboard on each shot. Make twenty shots.

Reverse Mikan Drill: Player starts under the basket, facing the court, and steps to the left side of the basket with his left foot, making a right hand reverse lay-up. He rebounds the ball and steps to the right side of the basket with his right foot, making a left hand reverse lay-up. Keep the ball above the shoulder level and complete without traveling. Make twenty.

Peth's Post Positioning Drill: One player begins on defense and the other on offense. Each whistle simulates a pass from the elbow extended to the baseline, thus requiring the defense to change his positioning, from ¾ front (or half front) on the high side to ¾ front (or half front) on the low side. The offense fights to hold his position while the defense fights to gain the proper positioning by making an X-step in front of the offensive player. Each player goes offensively for one minute and defensively for one minute. Repeat if necessary.

Block2Block Post Move Drill: With a partner, place balls at each of the blocks. Shooter runs to first block, picks up ball, establishes position and makes a post move. After converting the basket, he sprints to the other side of the lane where he repeats the same. Partner grabs the first rebound and sets it back on the block. Do for one minute each for each post move. In a three person group, have one player play defense.

Chapter 8:
The Training Stage

Age: 13-15
Objective: Refine basketball-specific skills, develop strength and fitness and expand tactical awareness in the 5v5 game.
Training to Competition Ratio: 60:40

Stage 3 (junior high school, freshman and junior varsity levels) is a transitory period between the preceding fun and learning and forthcoming competition. Continue development and refine skills with an increased intensity and competitiveness to prepare for Stage 4. Each level is a preparatory level, not an end: junior high school basketball prepares the athlete for high school basketball; the freshman and junior varsity prepare athletes for varsity basketball. "The reason why so many athletes plateau during the later stage of their careers is primarily because of an over-emphasis on competition instead of training during this period in their athletic development," (Balyi and Hamilton, 2003). Coordinate general athletic abilities with basketball-specific skills to enhance the player's basketball ability.

During this stage is the "window of accelerated adaptation to aerobic and strength training," (Balyi and Hamilton, 2003). Athletes hit their major growth spurt or the onset of Peak Height Velocity. "Optimal aerobic trainability begins with the onset of PHV," (Balyi and Hamilton, 2003). Train the aerobic system through intervals. "There are two windows of accelerated adaptation to strength training for females. Window one is immediately after PHV and window two begins with the onset of menarche (the first menstrual period). This window for males begins 12-18 months after PHV," (Balyi and Hamilton, 2005). Include resistance training during this period. Many believe athleticism is genetic; however, a careful development plan increases each athlete's athleticism and improves his opportunity to reach his optimal performance level. During the second and third stage, we "make or break an athlete...Athletes who miss this phase of training will not reach their full potential," (Balyi and Hamilton, 2003).

This stage is essential to a player's growth and ultimate development, yet many ignore the preparatory stages completely and view high school sports as one competitive stage, which is why athletes peak during this stage. Teams prepare to win; they do not prepare to improve. And, there is a significant difference, though commonly misunderstood, and this difference impedes players' development during the high school years.

Athletic Skills

Athletic Skills Training Goals: Strength, aerobic conditioning, power
Emphasis: Interval training, resistance training, power training, separation of the recreational players and serious competitors.

The Training Stage links the learning stages which precede it with the forthcoming competition stage; incorporates the previously learned and developed skills; and increases the training load and intensity in preparation for more intense and competitive training. Proper athletic development facilitates the Training Stage; athletes and teams with skill deficiencies require remedial training before progressing to Stage 3 training. For instance, if an athlete lacks the proper squatting technique, he needs a remedial program before he starts resistance training. Athletes lacking proper skill development lag behind as the increased training load and intensity intensifies the need for a sound fundamental base.

In the Training Stage, the increased load and intensity means training outside of the on-court practice. Unless players play multiple sports (which should be encouraged), athletes participate year-round, whether with the high school or a club team, which separates the competitive and the recreational player; each works hard on the floor, but the serious player trains away from basketball practice.

Periodization is an important training concept; it breaks the training year or season into different periods and cycles to prevent athlete burnout and overtraining and assist coaches in planning. The macrocycle is one training session or year; for an Olympic athlete, a macrocycle could cover four years though for most teams and athletes, the macrocycle is one season. A mesocycle is 21-28 days and a microcycle is a training week, or 7-10 days. The cycles insure a balanced training with appropriate themes, rest and regeneration. Currently, little thought is given to rest or peaking in the postseason.

Four periods comprise a macrocycle: Preseason Period, Competition Period, Rest/Transition Period and Off-season Period. For shorter youth leagues or if the majority of players play multiple sports, the Off-season and Pre-season can be combined into one Preparatory Period.

The Pre-season runs from the start of practice to the first game. However, a coach can manipulate the schedule to meet his objectives. While basketball runs from November to March, teams often start workouts in September. Therefore, a coach can use September-November as the Pre-Season Training or as Off-Season Preparation with the beginning of official practice in November commencing Pre-Season Training.

The Competition Period runs through the actual season, though coaches manipulate the specifics. During this time, teams train to peak for the postseason.

The Active Rest/Transition Period is a short period after the season ends when players get away from basketball and recover from the competitive season. This period is typically 2-4 weeks in a year-round program, but can be extended as needed. While many high school players rush from the high school season into club basketball, they do their bodies and their health a disservice. Rest is an important component in the training schedule.

The Off-Season runs through most of the spring and summer; for youth leagues, there is no off-season period; also, for many high school players, the off-season is the opportune time to play another sport. The off-season is a preparatory period before the more intense pre-season and in-season training.

Within the macrocycle and different periods are mesocycles, which last between 21-28 days, the approximate time it takes for the body to adapt to a training stimulus. After a period of rest or a week of unloading, the athlete begins another mesocycle and the body super-compensates; that is, the rest allows the body to grow and build muscle.

Each mesocycle has a theme. For instance, if school starts in September and practice officially starts in November, the coach divides the Pre-Season Period into two mesocycles. During the first cycle, athletes build a base level of strength and aerobic fitness. During the second cycle, athletes emphasize speed and power.

Within each mesocycle are microcycles which last 7-10 days but are usually thought of as a training week. Within the training week, the coach plans the sessions in advance and balances the intensity and volume. Intensity is the effort level; a game is maximum intensity while a jog might be 50% intensity. Numerically, an athlete who maxes 100lbs lifts 70lbs if the workout asks for sets at 70% intensity. Volume is the amount of work; for instance, 3 sets of 10 repetitions. As intensity increases, volume decreases; as the season progresses, practice sessions decrease in time.The intensity, volume and training goals determine the rest required; when doing a speed workout, work at 90% intensity with full recovery; however, during a speed endurance workout, train at 70% intensity with an incomplete recovery (1:1 or 1:2 work to rest ratio).

Movement Skills

The Dynamic Warm-up continues to refine and maintain proper movement patterns and increase dynamic flexibility. Incorporate additional drills into the warm-up to emphasize a particular skill. One day, emphasize lateral movement and add additional lateral drills, like a lateral skip, lateral bound or other exercises. On another day, train running stride technique with *Wall Drills* or *Partner Resistance Running*. Running seems like a simple, natural skill; however, last season, we designed a remedial running program for a junior college athlete because her poor running form contributed to speed deficiency and persistent knee problems. While these drills appear simplistic or irrelevant, nothing is more important to basketball success than quick and efficient movement.

Endurance

This is the stage of optimal aerobic conditioning. However, avoid cross country. Many believe cross country is great preparation for basketball; however, the transfer is minimal. Basketball is a quick, explosive game; cross country runs are slow, steady runs of distance. While a basketball player covers a couple miles in a basketball game, the running is short sprints interspersed with walking, jogging and standing.

Use interval training for basketball conditioning. *Shuttle Runs* add a change of direction dimension to the training. Modify the distance and rest time to train different components; to train speed endurance, run a longer distance (300m) at a lower intensity (80%) with a shorter rest interval (1:1); to train acceleration, run a shorter distance (20m) at a higher intensity (95%) with a longer rest interval (10:1).

Resistance Training

Follow two basic principles when designing a resistance training program: start from the inside-out and lift for power. Core (the muscles which attach to the spine and pelvis) strength stabilizes the body; furthermore, the core transfers power from the lower to the upper body and originates movement. Core strength is vital to overall strength; incorporate functional training concepts into the resistance training program to work the entire core.

Lifting for power emphasizes explosive lifts, such as a snatch or power clean, as opposed to traditional weight lifting workouts like bench, bicep curls and flys. "There must be sufficient power-related training during an athlete's early years (13-17) to maintain the genetically determined level of white (fast-twitch or power-related) muscle fiber. Power-related work also promotes the shift of transitional fiber to power-related muscle fiber," (Boyle). Depending on preference or experience, athletes use medicine balls, plyometrics and Olympic lifts to train explosively. Trainers/coaches unfamiliar with training techniques should study (I recommend the US Weightlifting Sports Performance Coach course to learn proper Olympic lifting techniques). Emphasize proper technique and weight room behavior to insure safety. Also, be cognizant of athletes' PHV (peak height velocity) and adjust training appropriately.

In Paul Check's *Movement that Matters*, he identifies six Primal Patterns; the basic movements of life: twist pattern, pull pattern, lunge pattern, push pattern, bend pattern and squat pattern. With these six patterns, develop a routine to supplement the power exercises. In all exercises, think functional; since basketball players play on their feet, train on the feet as much as possible. Rather than a leg press, leg extension and leg curl, incorporate a squat (squat pattern), lunge (lunge pattern) and straight-leg dead lift (bend pattern). Start with body weight, learning the correct form and progress to more difficult exercises, which may or may not include weight. For instance, the lunge progression might go: front lunge; reverse lunge; front-to-back lunge; back lunge off a step; 45-degree lunge; 45-degree back lunge; walking lunge holding a weight plate overhead. The lunge may be a theme through a macro cycle and each meso cycle incorporates a progressively more difficult lunge.

To train the upper body, emphasize the push, pull and twist patterns. The pull pattern is a pull-up, chin-up or reverse push-up. The push pattern is a push-up, which uses the core to stabilize the body. The squat, lunge and SDL work the core as well. For the twist movement, use a diagonal plate raise; take a weight plate or medicine ball (an appropriate weight) and lift the weight from the left knee to above the right shoulder, keeping the elbows straight. Work both sides.

To add additional core work, practice a bridge and side bridge: in the bridge, the athlete rests on his elbows and toes and stabilizes his body in a straight line, pulling his belly button to his spine. A side bridge uses only one elbow and foot, and the athlete is perpendicular to the floor.

This basic resistance plan emphasizes the core and body weight exercises, utilizes power-related lifts, teaches proper weight lifting technique and builds functional strength for young athletes as they prepare to enter the next stage, which features more intense workouts.

Tactical Skills

Goals: Open court decision-making; attacking defenders; off-ball movement; defensive rotations.
Emphasis: Transition basketball; decision-making.

Stages 1 and 2 prepare players for more advanced instruction. In Stage 3, refine previously learned tactical skills and develop principles to organize the attack.

If Stage 3 has one major emphasis, it is transition basketball. At this age, athletes develop a strong aerobic base and develop anaerobic fitness and power. Therefore, the running game fits perfectly into Balyi's model, as athletes handle greater levels of training stress, such as full court transition basketball.

Transition basketball starts with 1v1 play and individual moves covered in *Technical Skills*. Use the *Foster 1v1 Drill* as a precursor to transition drills, which start with the 2v1 fast break and continue to 5v5 transition play. Designing game-like transition drills is challenging because transition play is unpredictable; one of my pet peeves is the 3v2 drill commonly used as a pre-game warm-up; offensive players make five or six passes before shooting, often passing to teammates who are flat-footed on the baseline with a poor angle for a shot. This drill has zero transfer to the game. Instead, use drills like *1v2-2v1, 2v1 Breakdown, Rabbit, Transition Progression, San Diego Transition D, Army Drill* and *Numbers Transition Drill.*

University of Tennessee Women's Basketball Coach Pat Summit says, "Basketball is a game of transition and transition basketball must be practiced." Teams create fast break situations through turnovers, long rebounds, great outlet passes, bad shot selection or great point guard play. Two schools of thought exist: the middle break and the sideline break. However, transition situations are not black and white, and cookie-cutting all breaks defeats transition basketball's objective: advancing the ball quickly down court to take advantage of the defense. Great transition teams commit to running, pass the ball unselfishly and attack aggressively with good spacing.

General Transition Guidelines

1. 2v1 is the desired break; try to turn every transition situation into a 2v1.
2. Finish all 2v1 breaks with a lay-up.
3. Ball handler attacks with a scorer's mentality, not a passer's. In a 2v1, the ball handler finishes at the basket unless the defender stops the ball completely; in a 3v2, the ball handler must be prepared to shoot the three if the defense stays back, or penetrate past the first defender.
4. Make the play early. Many players take one or two too many dribbles.
5. Spacing is critical. In a 2v1, attack wider than the lane-lines; in a 3v2, wings get wide; in a four or five man break, space in width and depth-one or two players trail beyond the initial rush and cut to gaps in the defense.
6. Always be the second man; if a teammate has a break away, never take the lay-up for granted. Be the second man down court in case he misses.

Some players play with preconceived "rules" for the fast break, as if the fast break is a set play. Basketball is a constantly changing environment; players need full speed, decision-making practice. The basketball gods never descended upon the hallowed hardwood with an edict stating all fast breaks must run through the middle and all ball handlers must jump stop at a designated point. These "rules" handicap players' ability to play. One team's "rule" may be to pass ahead. However, in one instance, the PG realizes his post has poor hands and few moves from the three-point line, so he attacks the basket and creates a chippie for the post. Strict obedience to a rule is not the desired outcome; good decision-making is the goal.

Well-coached teams play well in transition. They pass the ball, attack and make good decisions; they understand the game, possess good habits and adjust to the situations. The coach empowers these players to play and perform.

Beyond the fast break, Stage 3 development includes more precise instruction on previously learned skills. More drills are used, as players make sense of the drills and transfer lessons to competition. At the next stage, the number of players drops, as teams grow more competitive and most teams cut players; therefore, player development and fun remain important, but build and nurture the competitive fire.

Stage 3 is hampered by too much instruction and not enough play or too much play and not enough instruction. Balance is the key. Drills are useful to introduce specifics and teach skills. For instance, when teaching a defensive close-out, use a drill to teach the movement, the small steps with weight back and hands extended, body prepared to move in any direction. However, once the skill is learned, use competitive repetitions to incorporate the skill. Too many teams spend the first half of practice drilling several skills and the second half scrimmaging. Instead, after teaching the proper stance and footwork, use a 1v1 drill to train decision-making and anticipation competitively using multiple repetitions. In games, skills do not breakdown; decision-making and communication breaks down. Players need repetitions training all aspects of the skill.

Teach and emphasize general principles in practice and games. Rather than implementing several plays, teach players the basics and empower players to make plays. Incorporate all previously learned skills into a more competitive, complex environment; take the basics, like getting open and passing against pressure, and add the general guidelines, like Diamond Spacing, to organize players and prepare for competition. In soccer, teams do not use set plays, except on dead ball situations; however, teammates need an expectation of how and where their teammates will move. Players play with guidelines or principles; for instance, if an offensive player dribbles toward the end-line, he expects teammates to make near-post and far-post runs and crosses the ball accordingly. Likewise, basketball players need organization-a set of expectations for teammates-and these guidelines offer an initial, loose structure which grows more sophisticated in the next stage.

General Offensive Principles

1. Pass and Move. An athlete's best opportunity to get open is as soon as he passes, as his defender follows the ball and/or relaxes.
2. A player is most open for a shot or move to the basket when he first receives the pass.
3. String Spacing: as a dribbler dribbles toward an offensive player, the offensive player flares away from the dribble forcing his defender to decide whether to help on the dribbler, leaving the offensive player open, or not help, leaving the ball handler's defender on an island; if the offensive player cannot flare any further (already near the sideline) he either loops behind the offensive player or cuts backdoor. As a dribbler one position away dribbles away from the offensive player, he follows to the vacated spot to maintain a passing angle.
4. If the ball goes to the baseline, either with a pass or dribble, the opposite wing drops to the baseline corner to give a passing lane.
5. If a ball handler dribbles toward a post player, the post circles away from the ball, keeping shoulders squared to the ball, to give space. If the dribble is toward the post's bottom foot, he makes an I-cut straight up the lane-line; if the dribble is toward the top foot, he circles to the baseline short corner.
6. Diamond Spacing. If a ball handler is trapped, his teammates form a diamond. One player is to his right (up the floor); one to his left (retreat pass/horizontal) and one straight ahead (splits the trap).

7. When using an off-ball screen, curl if the defender trails; flare if the defender goes high side/ball side; cut back door if the defender gets between the cutter and the screener; make a straight cut if the defender tries to fight through the screen. Screener rolls opposite the cutter; if the cutter goes to the basket, the screener goes high; if the cutter goes high, the screener rolls to the basket.
8. When using an on-ball screen, use two dribbles to spread the defense unless the ball handler turns the corner to the basket. If the defense hedges, traps or switches, and the ball handler cannot split the defense, use two dribbles to extend the defense.
9. Little offense on big defense is a better mismatch than little defense on big offense.
10. Triangle spacing. Against a zone, position oneself in a triangle with the two nearest defenders to add indecision as to which defender closes out. As a zone defender, the fastest person to the ball takes it; if two defenders end up at the ball, trap it.

Defensively, instruction depends greatly on each coach's system. Some teams pressure the ball, others contain; some deny all passes, others emphasize help. However, some general defensive principles are constants.

General Defensive Principles

1. Head on a swivel; see ball and man at all times.
2. When the ball moves, everybody moves. When your man moves, you move.
3. Communicate. Every player needs to communicate. Use small catch phrases.
4. Influence sideline-baseline in the half court. Weak side rotation must step in front of posts to eliminate interior pass and offensive rebounds if the post leaves to help.
5. Contest every shot. Force players to dribble into their shot: do not allow catch and shoot.
6. Possession does not end until defense gets the rebound. Everyone blocks out and rebounds.
7. Do not get split. Do not allow the player between his defender and the help defender.
8. Deny cutter outside the paint. Step from a help side, pistol position into denial position and bump the cutter before he enters the paint. Never let a player cut towards the ball without being denied.
9. In transition, retreat to the key keeping vision on the ball. Build the defense from the inside, out.

The *Shell Drill*, *Scramble* and *Seminole D* are three drills used to teach and train team defense as a whole, especially the important rotations when an initial defender is beaten, either off the dribble or due to a double-team in the post. Beyond these general principles, each coach decides his defensive system, and defensive instruction varies accordingly, especially as players move from the third to the fourth stage. Scouting and defensive preparation is emphasized more heavily in stage 4 and beyond.

In every situation, competition or live play follows drills. Drills exist as teaching tools; however, live play is like a pre-test. In math class, the teacher does not explain a concept, give some homework and then give the graded exam; the teacher explains the concept (instruction), gives homework (drills/repetitions), gives a pre-test or end of chapter test (live play) and then the exam (game). The live play can be a small-sided or full scrimmage, depending on the skills one is emphasizing and the time available. 3v3 remains the optimal game and a useful component for training, to simulate the game and transition players from drills to 5v5 play with additional repetitions against live (unpredictable) defense.

Regardless of level, coaches need to understand the skills they want to teach and give appropriate time to developing these skills. Stage 3 includes a wide spectrum of tactical skills; the introduction occurs during stage 3, but the instruction and development continues through stage 4. If the model is executed properly, stage 4 is more about refinement of previously introduced skills, as opposed to the introduction of new concepts.

Technical Skills

Technical Skills Training Goal: Create attack-minded players, advance previously learned skills.
Emphasis: Creativity, training skills for game-play, adding intensity to the drills and speed of skills.

The Training Stage advances previously introduced skills, nurtures attack-minded, aggressive players and incorporates basic skills into game-specific situations. Offensively, cultivate the Hard 2 Guard Mentality. Defensively, develop aggressive, smart defenders who understand situations and take advantage of the offense's weaknesses (individual defense is mostly an athletic and psychological skill, while team defense is largely a tactical skill).

During the Training Stage, Tactical Skill Training nurtures players' decision-making skills; Technical Skill development complements this training by insuring players possess the requisite skills and confidence in the skills to exploit these mental skills.

I. The Hard 2 Guard Mentality

In baseball, a great pitcher controls the game unless he makes a mistake (gets behind in the count, hangs a curveball, etc.). All pitchers are hittable, but a great pitcher dominates the hitters. A Hard 2 Guard player maintains similar control, despite the defense's attempts to eliminate options. University of Florida Head Coach Billy Donovan says, "Great offense beats great defense."

When players play one-on-one, the offensive player has the advantage. However, when more players are added, we favor the defense. While basketball is played 5v5, plenty of 1v1 action occurs. Unfortunately, most players catch the ball and believe they are guarded. Hard 2 Guard players see one defender and understand they possess the advantage: one defensive player cannot stop a player like Kobe, AI or King James; they have the ability, but, more importantly, the mindset. They force the defense to stop them.

This is not an invitation for selfish play, frivolous dribbling or dominating the ball. However, players must make themselves difficult to guard. They must be operational, look to create scoring opportunities and attack the defense. They must possess the mindset that an individual player cannot stop them. The attitude, confidence and mindset separate the good players from the great players.

Being Hard 2 Guard is an attitude. The confidence to make a move or take the shot, to know more than anything else in the world that one can score, is the most important attribute. Players like Dwyane Wade, Kobe and Steve Nash separate from the pack because of their mental approach, their fearlessness, and their confidence. An aggressive, attacking attitude puts fear in the opposition. A strong understanding of how to defeat various defenses and a strong mental preparation leads to a successful Hard 2 Guard player.

II. Shooting

The Training Stage incorporates the proper shooting mechanics (Stage 2) into game-like shooting, emphasizing the shooting footwork. The most important aspect when shooting on the move is acquiring balance before the shot; many players bend improperly and thus lean forward as they shoot. Sit back and bend by pushing one's hips back to gain balance; imagine the butt as the anchor: drop the anchor to stop.

Start the shooting progression by moving in a straight line to the basket. Use a stride stop. Next, curl toward the ball; use an inside foot stride stop. Use the *Circle Drill* to teach players the proper footwork and *Elbow Shooting Drill* to practice shots off a curl. Finally, practice shooting off the dribble while moving to the basket (*Straight Line Pull-ups* and *One-Dribble Pull-ups*). Proper footwork facilitates better balance and a quicker shot; instruct, train and emphasize footwork and balance when shooting, as correct lower body execution ameliorates correct upper body mechanics. Practice game shots from game spots at game speed.

III. Ball Handling

As players develop better moves, quickness and control with the ball, increase their ball handling arsenal. The four additional change of direction moves are:

- **Spin Dribble:** Used against body contact. While going right to left, plant the right foot and execute a reverse pivot. Take the ball with you: spin with your left hand on top of the ball, dribbling the ball while protected from the defense. Seal the defender and explode towards the basket.
- **Through-the-Legs:** Like a crossover, except the front leg protects the ball from the defender's reach. If dribbling from right to left, step forward with the left leg and bounce the ball behind the left foot.
- **Behind-the-Back (pull back):** To protect the ball, crossover behind the back. If going right to left, plant right foot and bounce the ball behind the left foot. Body and ball move together, so the player moves slightly to the left.
- **Around-the-back (open court):** Wrap the ball around the back, bouncing the ball on the side of the foot and pushing the ball forward, not straight down. If going right to left, plant left foot at defender and pull the ball around the back to the left side.

IV. Post Play

Practice a go-to move and a counter to each shoulder and increase a player's repertoire of moves and speed of execution. Train moves against contact, finishing through a defensive player. Focus on finishing with shoulders squared to the baseline, not the basket to protect the shot from the defense. Learn to fend off defenders with the inside hand without extending to draw a foul call. Train moves from a step off the block, short corner and high post; work on passing out of a double team and splitting defenders to get to the basket.

Four basic moves are:

- **Drop Step Power Lay-up**: Drop bottom foot toward the basket and seal the defender. Use one dribble, gather with shoulders parallel to the backboard and finish with a power lay-up.
- **Step Middle Jump Hook**: Step to the middle of the floor with the top foot, attempting to seal the defender's top foot. Dribble and gather on two-feet, with inside shoulder pointed to the rim and shoot a jump/baby hook.
- **McHale Up And Under**: Step to the middle of the floor with the top foot, gather, show the ball high and step through and past the defensive player to the basket.
- **Quick Spin** (verse an aggressive defender leaning on the offensive player): Make a quick, front pivot on the baseline foot and step to the basket; extend with the dribble. Use the elbow on the turn to nudge the defense away from the basket. Finish with a power lay-up or a reverse lay-up.

Stage 3 Drills

Athletic Skills

Wall Drill: Place hands against the wall to create a power position with body in a straight line, but angled toward the wall. Run in place, driving the knees up. Start with 2 strides and build.

Partner Resistance Running: Partner places hands against the runners shoulders and the runner leans into the the partner to create the power position. As the partner provides resisitance, the runner drives his legs and runs down the court.

Shuttle Run: Place three cones five meters apart. Start at the middle cone; run to one cone, then to the far cone and to the middle cone to complete the 5-10-5 shuttle run.

Tactical Skills

Foster 1v1 Drill: Offensive player starts on the baseline and the defensive player starts at the free throw line with the ball. Defensive player passes the offensive player the ball, sprints to half court, turns and picks up the offensive player, attempting to keep the offensive player to the sideline and away from the paint. Defensive player must force the offensive player to change directions, and not just run right past the defender.

1v2-2v1: This drill trains ball handling under pressure, sudden change from offense to defense and the 2v1 transition opportunity. One player starts on offense and two players start on defense. The offensive player attempts to advance the ball up court and jump stop in the key for a shot; the defense traps and prevents the offensive player from advancing the ball. On a change of possession (made basket, rebound, steal, violation), the two defenders become the offensive player and the offensive player becomes a single defensive player.

Rabbit: Teams line up along opposite sidelines; the first team, Team A, starts with two offensive players at half-court and its first defender protecting its basket; Team B starts with one defender protecting its basket. As soon as Team A crosses half-court, the second player from Team B sprints to the center of the circle and then retreats to help his teammate: the 2v1 fast break becomes a 2v2 game. Offense remains on offense until the defense rebounds or steals the ball; if the offense scores, they get their own rebound and score again. Once B gets the ball, they attack 2v1 against A's first defender; the second A defender enters when B crosses half-court. Game is played to seven points.

2v1 Breakdown: Defense starts at the free throw line with the ball and offensive players start on the baseline. Defensive player passes to one of the offensive players and back pedals to half court. The offense advances the ball with the pass until half court and then attacks 2v1 from half court.

Numbers Transition: Players start on the baseline in a single file line; five players are involved in every series. Drill starts with the coach tossing the ball out toward the other basket. Player 1 runs for the ball and attempts to score a lay-up on the other end. Player 2 is a defensive player, attempting to stop P1. Player 3 sprints to the half court circle and then to the opposite free throw line-extended to become an outlet to take the ball in the other direction. Player 4 sprints to the half court circle and then to the free throw line-extended on the opposite side of the court from P3. Player 5 sprints to the half court circle and then back pedals as a defender. After P1 scores, P2 inbounds the ball with a quick pass to P3 or P4. P1 immediately sprints back on defense and teams with P5. P2, P3 and P4 attack in a 3 v 2 fast break. Once the play is finished, the sixth person in line starts as P1 and the drill continues; if there are fewer than ten players, players must jump immediately into line and be ready to join the drill as soon as the first series ends.

Army Drill: Drill starts with 3-5 offensive players across the baseline and 3-5 defensive players across from them along the free throw line extended. Throw the ball to one of the offensive players: the offense takes off toward their basket on a fast break. The corresponding defensive player (player across from player who received the ball) must touch the baseline and then get back on defense. All other defensive players must get back to stop the fast break and slow offense until the defensive player recovers.

Transition Progression: Play begins with nine players in the key; five blue offensive players and four red defensive players. Coach tosses the ball to a Blue player and the Red defenders retreat while the Blue offensive players attack in a five-on-four fast break. Once the Blue team shoots, the shooter and the passer step off and the other three Blue players sprint back on defense; the four Red defenders secure the rebound and attack offensively in a four-on-three break. Once again, the Red passer and shooter step off to create a three-on-two advantage for the Blue and then the Blue passer and shooter step off to create a two-on-one for the Red. To make it competitive, play a game, giving each team a shot to start with the ball. This is a quick drill and forces the offense to communicate as soon as they shoot the ball, as often the point guard who would normally be the safety is the passer or shooter and therefore is emptying out of the drill. The other players must be aware and protect their basket.

San Diego Transition D: Team 1 starts on offense with Player 1 shooting a free throw and Player 2 lined up as a rebounder on the lane line. Team 2 has three players lined up along the lane line to rebound. P1 shoots and Team 2 rebounds the miss or inbounds the make and attacks three-on-two; two Team 1 players wait under their defensive basket. After Team 2 scores or Team 1 rebounds/steals the ball, Player 3 and Player 4 join P1 and P2 and attack the three Team 2 players in a four-on-three break; two new Team 2 players wait under their defensive basket. After Team 1 scores or Team 2 rebounds/steals, the two new players join the three Team 2 players and attack in a five-on-four fast break; the final Team 1 player waits under the defensive basket. After Team 2 scores or Team 1 rebounds/steals the ball, the Player 5 joins Team 1 and the two teams play five-on-five until someone scores.

Shell Drill: The most commonly used team defense drill. Start with four offensive players around the perimeter and four defensive players matched up against each one. As the offensive players swing the ball, defenders sprint and adjust positioning; when the ball is moved, every player must move and position himself in relation to the ball: defenders one pass away should have a hand in the passing lane and those two passes away should be in help position. After players understand proper positioning in relation to the ball, allow offensive players to cut to the basket. Defenders now must deny the basket cuts and then assume proper positioning. In the third stage, allow dribble penetration baseline, so defenders must help to stop the ball and help defenders must rotate to cover easy lay-up opportunities and force the pass back to the three-point line. After players master the rotations, add a fifth offensive and defensive player in the post. Teach defense positioning (whatever the particular scheme, front, behind, three-quarter front) for the post defenders and also the wing defenders; how to help, how to double, rotations out of the double team. Eventually work to play the drill live.

Seminole D: Drill used to build enthusiasm and pride in getting defensive stops. In a normal scrimmage situation, score offensive points normally, but give the defense five points (or more) for a stop. If and when either team leads by more than five points, give the trailing team the choice of playing defense or offense. If teams continue to stay on offense (and some will because they know they can't stop anybody defensively), increase the amount of points for a defensive stop. The idea is to reward the stronger defensive team and illustrate how defensive stops can win games, regardless of offensive output.

Scramble: This is a defensive 5-on-4 drill with no offensive restrictions. Defense must hold offense without a shot for a period of time (10 seconds). Drill works mini-transition and also team defense when a player is beaten off the dribble and play does not go into the "shell" form. The top player must cover the ball; the next two players match-up with the next most serious scoring threats and the fourth defensive player plays the weak side, shading towards the basket.

Technical Skills

Circle Drill: Players form a circle around a target/basket. They start jogging to their right and when the coach gives the command "Shot," all players jump off their inside foot and square to the target in shooting position, with imaginary ball ready to shoot. On the "Go," command, they run in the other direction, and repeat, squaring to the target on command. If players work on a 1-2 step, have players plant the inside foot on the "Shot," command and square to the target with the plant and pivot.

Elbow Shooting Drill: With two players, Player 1 is shooter and Player 2 rebounds. P1 starts by receiving ball at elbow and shoots the ball. P2 rebounds. P1 runs along the half-circle above the free throw line to the other elbow, receives pass and shoots. Shoot ten and then rotate. The point of the drill is to work on stepping into the ball with a 1-2 step off of the inside foot. Players should be comfortable shooting with either foot as their pivot foot.

Straight Line Pull-ups: Sprint toward the basket in a straight line, catch and shoot. Work from different spots on the floor.

One Dribble Pull-ups: Player 1 shoots, Player 2 passes and Player 3 is a token (three-quarter speed) defender. P2 makes the skip pass to P1, and P3 closes-out to defend the initial move (defender stops on the dribble). P1 makes a shot fake (ball to eyes) and extends away from the defender with one dribble and pulls up for a jump shot. Initially, have the defense closeout to force a certain direction; a couple shots to the baseline and a couple to the middle. Eventually, allow the defender to closeout without instruction so the offensive player must read the defense when making his move. Passer becomes the next defender, defender becomes the next shooter and shooter follows his shot, rebounds and takes the ball to the passing line.

Chapter 9:
The Competition Stage

Age: 16-18 (Varsity Basketball)
Objective: Build the competitive fire, optimize basketball skills, specialize position skills and build the team first mentality.
Training to Competition Ratio: 40:60

The development model diverges in Stage 4, as competition increases. Stage 4 is high school varsity basketball; for many athletes, varsity basketball is the pinnacle of their competitive career; they may play Intramurals in college or in recreation leagues as adults, but competitive adult basketball (college/professional) is not in their future; others drop out of the competitive mix, by choice or by cut, and play recreationally; for the elite, Stage 4 is another step toward the ultimate goal, which is the Performance Stage, college and professional basketball. A varsity coach juggles different interest, ability and commitment levels.

At this level, training sessions are highly competitive; teaching continues, but more coaching occurs, as strategy increases. Every day includes basic fundamentals, but the emphasis is varsity game preparation and success, not mastering fundamentals, which occurs during the previous stages.

At the varsity level, games matter; individuals subjugate their games for the good of the team; and players specialize skills and positions. For most athletes, building the competitive fire translates directly towards the competitive season; however, for elite athletes, building the competitive fire creates additional motivation to succeed at the highest levels.

Team drills revolve around the team's system of play; some teams play fast and some play slow; some shoot outside shots, some pass the ball until they get a lay-up; some defend full court, some drop into a zone. Practice decisions depend largely on the team's style of play, as a zone team trains differently than a team that presses. Players require time to master and gain confidence in the team's system and to play with one another to learn tendencies, strengths and weaknesses.

If players develop the skills as outlined through the model, coaches can implement more creative, liberal systems utilizing the players' knowledge and ability on the court, rather than restricting movement in a robot-like set. Properly developed players advance basketball and its strategy.

Athletic Skills

Athletic Skills Training Goal: Power, acceleration, vertical jump, dynamic balance, functional strength.
Emphasis: Prepare for competitions, train for peak performance, and elevate one's training to the next level.

The Training Stage transitions athletes from learning to competition by increasing training loads and intensity; in the Fourth Stage, training load and intensity increase further and specificity increases. In the first three stages, athletes train to improve athleticism, as increased overall athleticism improves basketball performance.

In Stage Four, training is basketball and position-specific; this stage capitalizes on the foundation and transforms athletic skills into basketball success.

During the Competition Stage, use testing to measure an athlete's progress and determine his weaknesses. Testing includes physical attributes such as height, weight and body fat percentage, as well as physiological attributes like vertical jump, broad jump, push-up test, shuttle run, etc. Measure results against elite players and determine one's strengths, weaknesses and training needs.

An athlete who has a low vertical jump may be weak in one of two areas: (1) his force production is low (strength) or (2) his movements are not explosive (power). If he scores well in quickness and a power-related test like the snatch, but his squat is low, the problem in his vertical jump is force; if he squats well, his weakness is explosiveness. If he needs to improve his force, his training emphasis is heavy squats; if he needs to improve his explosiveness, his training protocol is more plyometrics. Testing improves training and increases individualization.

At this stage, the Dynamic Warm-up is a short warm-up. An additional warm-up idea is stations. A five station warm-up would be: (1) Jump rope; (2) Speed ladder; (3) Lane-line slides; (4) Push-ups; and (5) medicine ball twists.

Movement

Movement training is part of the technical and tactical development, as players learn to move while executing skills or within the team's framework. Emphasize a low body posture on offensive moves to accelerate with the first step and proper force application on lateral movement. Periodically, review these concepts away from basketball skills.

At an elite camp, I worked with a high school senior who did not know how to move laterally or backwards. She wanted to play major DI basketball, but plays in the Ivy League because most programs said she was too slow defensively. Her foot speed was not the problem; her insufficient skill development made her slow. Once she learned to hop backward on an offensive player's first move to create space and push in the direction she wanted to go, her defense improved and she was quicker. More emphasis on athletic skill execution translates to better basketball movement.

Resistance Training

As strength and power increases, add more exercises, vary exercises and increase the functionality of exercises. Many functional exercises incorporate balance and increase ankle tendon and ligament strength, which protects against ankle sprains. An example is to stand on one leg while doing the diagonal plate raise.

In this stage, players add more exercises to complement their routines; for upper body lifts, do a horizontal and vertical push and pull exercise. An example of a vertical pull is a pull-up; a horizontal pull is a bent over row. An example of a horizontal push is a push-up, while a vertical push is a military press.

As strength increases in the lower body, work on single-leg strength. Most basketball movements are single leg movements, so train legs individually: move from a squat to a split squat to a raised split squat to a single-leg squat. When making an aggressive cut, the leg decelerates much like a single-leg squat; the additional strength through training each leg individually reduces the injury risk when planting and cutting.

Through this development model, athletes gain requisite strength (double and single leg) and movement skills (landing, stopping) to perform high intensity plyometric exercises like box jumps and explosive Olympic lifts like the snatch. Instruct proper weightlifting technique and demand athletes follow the rules to insure everyone's safety, but the goal is better basketball performance. Modify lifts to meet the athletes' needs. If a coach/athlete is uncomfortable with the snatch or power clean, use a hang start (knees, not the floor) or change the exercise: use a jump shrug, high pull or medicine ball throw to work on explosive hip action. Manage each athlete's volume and intensity and progress gradually.

At this age, workouts require periodization. In the off-season, train hypertrophy; add muscle mass to growing frames; for conditioning, build the anaerobic base. In the pre-season, train power, adding quickness and explosiveness for the season, while conditioning builds speed and acceleration. During the season, train for injury prevention. The training stimulus changes accordingly to enhance overall performance and overcome plateaus.

Important with these concepts is rest and gradual progressions. Within each mesocycle, the athlete progresses in intensity for 2-3 weeks (as intensity increases, volume decreases) and then unloads or reduces the intensity for a week to allow the body to adapt. Without rest, the body does not adapt and players do not progress as rapidly, which leads to frustration and overtraining.

Basketball Physiology

Basketball is an anaerobic sport requiring a high percentage of fast-twitch, Type II muscle fiber: basketball requires high force production (Type IIb) and high power output (Type IIa and Type IIb). Basketball is a running sport, but the running occurs in short, powerful bursts with quick starts and stops and repetitive jumps and landings. "Aerobic endurance demands…are minimal…a typical NBA game…in the first half the ball was in play for an average of 49.1 seconds before action paused for an average of 35.3 seconds. In the second half, the average time of non-stop action was 37.5 seconds, with the average pause being 58.9 seconds," (Gambetta).

The phosphagen system and anaerobic glycolysis supply the energy to meet basketball's metabolic demands. The phosphagen system provides energy for fast and powerful movements, as in a full court sprint, a quick change of direction or a maximum jump for a rebound. As intense exercise extends beyond 8-10 seconds, anaerobic glycolysis provides the body's energy. In an up-tempo game, with few breaks and sustained maximum output, glycolysis supplies the energy. One characteristic of glycolysis is lactate acid build up; therefore, a basketball player must train his/her system to tolerate higher levels of lactate acid in the blood.

No single energy system provides all the energy for a specific exercise. "Integrating the two metabolic demands is also a vital training need because many athletes must be able to perform under fatiguing conditions in competition. Nevertheless, each metabolic component needs to be trained individually for optimal results, and then both need to be combined in sport-related training," (Baechele).

Long distance training is contraindicated because training slow reduces explosiveness: to excel in basketball, train fast to meet metabolic demands and develop Type IIa and IIb muscle fibers. "[Speed expert Charlie] Francis believed that not only can you make an athlete into a sprinter, but, more important, that you might negatively affect an athlete's ability to develop speed by focusing on endurance," (Boyle).

Basketball is a multi-directional game; linear training (running straight ahead) alone is insufficient; train for the metabolic demands of quick stops and starts and prepare the muscles, ligaments and tendons for quick changes of directions. When designing a basketball conditioning program, include short interval runs and shuttle runs which emulate basketball's demands. A well-rounded conditioning program incorporates all aspects, but emphasizes multi-direction skills, acceleration and short runs (10-30m).

Tactical Skills

Goals: Mental skills, strengths/weaknesses, team strategy, competitiveness, skill application.
Emphasis: Refine and enhance skills, utilize players' strengths and capitalize on technical skill development.

Tactical skill development combines the previous lessons into an effective attack based on the team's personnel. Coaches organize the attack, place players in position to succeed and emphasize the personnel's strengths while managing its weaknesses. In earlier stages, all teams (theoretically) learn and practice similar skills. In Stage 4, coaches emphasize certain skills based on the team's strengths and weaknesses. A team with a great point guard may emphasize the screen and roll and concentrate on floor spacing and stand-still, spot-up shooting. A team of shooters may emphasize constant motion, off-ball screens, shooting and precision passing. Continue to develop all skills, but concentrate on a small spectrum to emphasize. In previous stages, the model insures a broad, skill-based development; in Stage 4, player development is more specific and sophisticated, narrowing the focus of each player to perform optimally in his role.

Competitive success requires continued development. With well-trained players, the continued learning is largely mental. Players not only understand the skill, but when and how to use the skill for the team's betterment. The speed of execution is as important as the precision of execution.

Develop mental skills through significant formal and informal play. Guide the process. Coaches develop and introduce the team's basic structure and system, and players play within the framework; different coaches have different philosophies, and coaches and players must communicate to optimize performance within each coach's framework. Some prefer up-tempo, fast break style of play with lots of three-point attempts; others prefer a slower pace and lots of post touches. Therefore, a good shot differs, and players must accept the coach's definitions and play within the team structure. Develop roles for each player; however, these roles should not limit players-"Never dribble the ball"-but position players to maximize their talent. Though the goal is to win, encourage players to play without fear of failure. Explain to each player his strengths and weaknesses and how he/she can help the team succeed.

Success in stage 4 depends on development in Stages 1-3. Without a strong fundamental base, players struggle to perform at the highest levels and depend heavily on coaches to tell them what to do on the court. However, through this development model, players prepare to play "real" basketball, an attacking, up tempo style of play which players and fans enjoy.

Stage 4 uses many of the same drills as earlier stages; however, the speed of execution and intensity of effort increases. A great variety of drills is not necessary, as training sessions require competitive play (1v1, 3v3 or 5v5) to measure players and build mental toughness. Team preparations demand significant attention as well, as teams scout and game plan for particular opponents. Finally, plan and practice game scenarios: end-game situations, how to hold a lead, how to come from behind, how to foul if needed, how to set-up a game winning shot, what to do in a tie game, etc.

Short-game scrimmages provide excellent training for different end-game situations. Use regularly to keep practices competitive and train for up-coming opponents. Scrimmaging with different situations (up three with thirty seconds to play; down two with fifteen seconds to play; down five with one minute to play, etc.) prepares players for competition; secondly, the in-practice competition builds the competitive fire.

Training at this level depends on the coach's particular system, the player's maturity, the player's prior basketball development and the team's personnel. Some coaches coach, while others teach. In an old ESPN.com article, analyst Jay Bilas differentiated coaching and teaching like this:

Generally, "coaching" consists of team preparation, the devising of game plans and schemes to defeat opponents. When you are coaching, you are dealing with strategies, different offenses and defenses, and putting in plays to take advantage of the skills, strengths and weaknesses of your players. The measure of a coach is the quality of the development of his system, and has been distilled into winning.

"Teaching" consists of instruction and training of individuals in the fundamental skills of the game, and in teaching players how to play, instead of how to run plays. The measure of a teacher is not in winning, but in the fundamental soundness and skill level of the players taught. A player with excellent fundamentals and skills can play successfully in any system.

At the varsity level, teams and players need a coach and teacher; in Stage 4, coaching and teaching are balanced. In Stages 1-3, emphasize teaching over coaching, while in Stage 5, coaching is emphasized over teaching.

Even in pursuit of victories, individual development, learning and fun should not be ignored. Elite players seeking an opportunity to play at the next level need to improve and diversify their games; others need continued improvement to increase confidence. While practices increase in intensity, training should be fun so players approach practice with a positive mindset because of the challenges presented; players should not dread practice nor feel bored at practice. Too many drills and dry running set plays undermine training as minds wander, improvement wanes and the challenges subside. While there are ebbs and flows, continually challenge players to maintain fun and motivation.

Technical Skills

Technical Skills Training Goal: Enhance and refine skills; prepare for game execution.
Emphasis: Competitive skills, playing to one's strengths and peak performance

Spend a significant amount of technical training playing 1v1, 2v2 or 3v3. Players with satisfactory and advanced skill development need training at game speed against live defense to hone their skills. Players with substandard skill development or a skill deficiency-such as a great PG with flawed shooting mechanics-require an individualized remedial program which identifies and addresses the individual's needs. Change is difficult; however, at this stage, a player's game plateaus if he has a flaw like poor shooting mechanics; additional practice is insufficient if he requires change to elevate his performance. To perform optimally, the athlete must develop better shooting technique through a program which focuses on the shooting lessons of stages 1-3.

Technical drills serve as conditioning drills and train multiple skills. A partner shooting drill like *Interval Curls* trains game-like shooting; conditions the athlete; and works on passing and receiving skills between the passer and shooter. Full court ball handling drills like the *Logger Drill* and post footwork drills like *Tap-Outlet-Finish* train game-specific conditioning.

During the course of a training week, or even every practice, use the basic instructions and drills covered in the initial three stages: players never outgrow fundamental training. Even when I coached professionally in Europe, we used the *Three in a Row Drill* every practice and started every post breakdown with the *Mikan Drill.*

University of South Carolina football coach Steve Spurrier believes there are *Everyday Drills*, which train basic fundamentals and should be used every day. Players never get too old or too good to practice the basics and those who spend the most time practicing basic fundamentals are typically the best players. During a recent San Antonio Spurs game, the commentator mentioned his surprise at seeing Tony Parker working on lay-ups with an assistant coach less than two hours before tip-off; the commentator said players typically practice only jump shots. But, Parker was rewarded with his first trip to the All-Star Game.

Make technical drills competitive to insure maximum effort and speed. Shooting drills like *30* train multiple shots from different spots and test shooting accuracy and speed. Other technical skill training involves position breakdown; use breakdown sessions to reinforce the team's system of play and general position-specific skills.

Point Guard

The point guard is the floor general and an extension of the coach. Beyond basic ball handling and shooting skills, point guards need a high basketball IQ; the position requires a thorough understanding of the game and the coach's philosophy. Use breakdown drills to work on handling traps (*1v2/2v1*); train penetrate and kick (*String Shooting, Berkeley Pass and Finish*); use the pick and roll; make decisions in transition (*3v2*); shoot off the dribble (*One Dribble Pull-ups*) and finish shots in the key.

Wing

Wing breakdown sessions train ball handling, creating one's own shot, shooting off cuts within the offense and passing into the post. Breakdown the proper way to set-up and use screens (straight cut, flare, curl, backdoor, etc.), as well as creating space without a screen. Work on individual live ball moves and creating space for a shot (pull-back jumpers). Train passing into the post with a *Block Passing Drill*.

Post

Post breakdown reinforces the general footwork and trains posts to get open and provide a passing lane for the wings. Also, players practice moves from spots where they frequently get the ball in games, whether off offensive rebounds, on the low block or in the short corner. Incorporate defense into most post drills as few interior shots occur without a defensive presence and reading and taking advantage of the defense is possibly the most important post skill to learn and the most difficult to teach.

Beyond position breakdown, skill refinement and conditioning, additional technical practice occurs through tactical training. Once technical skills reach a satisfactory performance level, the next step is game application, which requires practicing skills in a game environment with multiple repetitions. The ability to perform skills in games and against defense is the focus of the Competition Stage, as technical and tactical skills are complimentary.

<h2 style="text-align:center">Stage 4 Drills</h2>

Tactical Skills

1v1: Play from different angles with different rules: play full court; start with defense in help and a skip pass; start with a point to wing entry pass; start with ball checked at half court, the three-point line, the block; limit the number of dribbles. Use the rules to emphasize instruction.

Technical Skills

Interval Curls: Shooter starts in the corner and curls toward the elbow. After each shot, jog to the baseline. Sprint into each shot. Make 3 shots and switch shooters.

Logger Drill: Place 6-7 chairs throughout the court, from free throw line to free throw line. Player must make 6 free throw line pull-up jumpers to complete the drill. While dribbling from end to end, the player must make an open court move (hard crossover, hesitation, in-and-out, around-the-back, through-the-legs) at a minimum of three chairs.

Tap-Outlet-Finish: Player 1 begins with ball in his hands doing backboard touches as high on the glass as possible. When Player 2 calls, "Ball," P1 pivots and fires a quick overhead pass to P2. After passing, P1 sprints to the other block; V-cuts back to the ball, receives a pass and finishes with a power move to the basket. He grabs the ball out of the net and resumes backboard touches.

1v2/2v1: Defense works together to trap and contain the ball handler. Trap the back pocket. Dribbler's goal is to beat the defense and jump stop in the offensive paint, assuring he/she is under control. On a steal (or basket), the offensive player retreats on defense, while the defenders attack on offense on a two-on-one break. Defense must work to create and keep the trap.

30: Player 1 is shooter and Player 2 rebounds. There are five spots on the floor and three shots in each series. The first shot in the series is worth three points, second shot is worth two points and third shot is worth one point. The five spots are the baseline on each side of the floor, forty-five degree angle on each side, and the top of the key. P1 starts under the basket and sprints to touch the sideline, then cuts towards the pass, receiving ball at three-point line for shot #1. P2 rebounds. After shooting, P1 must return and touch the sideline, then cut towards the ball. After receiving pass, P1 must execute a shot fake, take one dribble and pull-up for shot #2. After shooting, he must run back and touch the sideline, then cut towards the ball, again receiving it at the three-point line. He must execute a shot fake, then make one dribble drive for a lay-up. After completing lay-up, he moves to next spot, touching the sideline near the hash mark and then cutting towards the basket. Continue through all five spots for a possible total of thirty points. The rebounder keeps track of shooter's total.

String Shooting (Flare): Passing line (with balls) starts on the wing, free throw line extended beyond the three-point line and shooting line starts at the top of the key. Passers penetrate middle, jump stop and pass to the shooter. The shooter creates space by flaring away from the dribbler to punish the help defense. Shooter follows his own shot and fills the line with the ball; passer fills the shooter line.

String Shooting (Follow): First person in passing line dribbles to the baseline, away from the Shooter, jump stops and passes the ball to the shooter. The shooter follows (keeping good spacing) and shoots. Again, shooter follows his shot and the players switch lines. The shooter must keep enough distance between he and the dribbler. Passers should work on a reverse pivot to pass the ball out, protecting the ball from the defense.

Berkeley Pass and Finish: PG starts at half-court with the ball and is played by a defensive player. One player begins in the key as a second defensive player and the other players form lines in either baseline corner. The PG's objective is to beat the top defender and then draw the second defender to the ball. Once the defender commits, the PG chooses one of the offensive players from the corner to pass the ball to. The player who receives the ball attempts a lay-up, while the one who does not receive a pass attempts to stop the other player from scoring.

3v2: Start with three offensive players at half court and two defenders protecting each basket. Other players fill lines at each basket. The three offensive players attack in a three-vs.-two fast break, looking to score quickly. If the offense scores, they get the ball out of the net and outlet the ball to the point guard and attack the other basket. If the defense gets a turnover or rebound, the two defenders outlet the ball to the middleman (point guard) and they attack the other basket. New players always enter on defense first, and the middleman/point guard remains the same, until the coach switches the point guard. As long as the offense scores, they stay on the court as offense; defenders must get a stop to play offense; otherwise, they go to the end of the line.

Chapter 10:
Basketball Coaches Training Program

Beyond the preceding four stage model for youth basketball development, United States basketball development requires better coaching education programs to assist and challenge coaches to continue learning and improving. Many professions require a certification for employment: hair stylists, bartenders, teachers, personal trainers, etc. To maintain a certification, personal trainers complete CEU's (Continuing Education Units), which educate trainers on the latest trends, promote professional advancement and broaden the trainer's knowledge. Asking coaches of a certain level or within a certain organization to maintain a professional certification is not a giant burden, and the professional growth is worth the effort.

Every coach is influenced, negatively or positively, by the coaches for whom they played or assisted. Using a former coach as a mentor is great for a young/novice coach; however, the coaches' training program challenges a coach not to coach exactly like his mentor, but to improve and develop his own coaching foundation and philosophy.

Basketball development suffers because coaches are content using the same instruction and drills they used as players; however as research and science evolves, the relevance and accuracy of some drills and instruction disappears. Ten years ago, popular opinion suggested static stretching prevented injuries; however, today, using static stretching as a warm-up is dubious, as research shows its an improper warm-up for a dynamic activity like basketball, and its usefulness is post-training, as part of the cool down. Unfortunately, many coaches regurgitate their coach's instructions without any critical thinking as to the best method.

The Basketball Coaches Training Program is designed to improve a coach's basic knowledge and understanding of the art and science of coaching basketball. While a Master's in Exercise Science gives a coach an advantage, it is not practical for every coach to possess an extensive scientific background, nor to exclude potential coaches without formal educations. I started coaching as a seventeen year old high school junior and believe strongly in the power of experience; however, my coaching and training improves annually as I study, learn and critically examine the game and teaching techniques. A basic foundation and continuing education is important for coaches, as better coaches using better training methodology develop better players. The BCTP is designed to teach the basics and provide a forum for more advanced continuing education.

Coaching is an art; teaching players, motivating players, criticizing players, managing a loss, building players' self-esteem, creating a positive team environment, developing a coaching philosophy, etc. Coaching is also a science; basic physiological and biomechanical principles govern training, as coaches can teach players to run faster, jump higher, land more safely, use energy more efficiently, etc. Coaching also involves basketball-specific aspects which combine the art and science. Making decisions on substituting and drawing up the final play are an art, while teaching the proper shooting form and designing a practice session, week and season is a science.

Most coaches and coaching literature focus on basketball's X's and O's and little emphasis is given to the art and science of coaching. Coaching education programs are a vital cog in the player development scheme; online retailers market hundreds of DVD's offering dozens of ways to attack a 2-3 match-up zone, but few address the science and foundation of basketball.

Within the United States Olympic Committee (USOC), each sport is governed by its national federation (USA Basketball). In theory, each national federation oversees amateur competition, training and coaching. Many federations, such as US Soccer, USA Track and Field, USA Weightlifting and US Swimming sponsor coaching education programs. For instance:

> U.S. Soccer's Coaching Education Department offers a wide range of educational opportunities for the certification and training of coaches. Currently more than 15,000 coaches are certified through our programs...The structure has been established for initial instruction courses (D, E, & Youth Modules) to be conducted in every state, leading up to four levels of certification held at the national level (A, B, C, & Youth License). These courses are held at regular intervals throughout the year at different sites and provide instruction and practical experience in all aspects of the game (www.ussoccer.com).

"C" License Course

The "C" License course provides continued instruction on the development of individual skill taught within individual and small group activities and games (4v4 to 7v7) and the understanding and development of tactics through 4v4 to 9v9 games. Additionally, this course is designed to train coaches to observe mistakes and make appropriate corrections. Testing includes oral, written and practical coaching evaluations.

A National "D" License held for 12 months is a prerequisite for this course and candidates must be 18 years old. A minimum of 5 years of coaching experience at an appropriate level is suggested.

I attended the initial certification courses offered by USA Weightlifting (Sports Performance Coach) and USA Track and Field (Level I). Each federation organizes its certifications and courses differently; however, USA Basketball absconds from coaching education programs, centering its attention on choosing teams for international competition. The schedule for the 21-hour USA Track and Field Level I course:

Saturday
7:30-8:30AM Registration/Introductions
8:30-9:30AM Philosophy, Ethics and Risk Management
9:30-11:00AM Physiology
11:00-12:00PM Biomechanics
12:00-1:00 Training Theory
1:00-2:30 Lunch
2:30-5:30 Throws Unit
5:30-7:30 Biomotor Training
7:30-8:30 Psychology

Sunday
8:00-9:00AM Endurance
9:00-12:00PM Sprints-Relays-Hurdles
12:00-1:00 Lunch
1:00-3:00PM Sprints-Relays-Hurdles
3:00-5:00PM Vertical Jumps
5:00-7:00PM Horizontal Jumps
7:00-7:30PM Wrap-up

To complete the Level I certification, attendees pass (80%) a 200 question take home exam. USATF offers a Level II and III certification; the Level II course is an intensive 8-day program, while Level III requires the applicant to produce an original paper and attend 3 21-hour advanced clinics.

Basketball Canada offers four courses through its National Coaching Certification Program:

Pre-level 1
This 4 hour course is designed for individuals coaching children aged 7-11. This course provides coaches with a solid understanding of basketball fundamentals. Coaches involved in Steve Nash Youth Basketball Leagues and other community based programs should consider taking this course.

NCCP Level 1
This one day course emphasizes individual skill development. Topics covered include socialization, skill analysis, footwork and dribbling, individual offense, rebounding, and dribbling. The NCCP Level 1 courses are usually held in the Spring and Fall. Cost for this course is $107.00 (incl. GST) which includes a manual and 6-8 hours of training.

NCCP Level 2
This course is designed for people coaching at the high school level. The course focuses on group skills. It provides coaches with skills and drills that can be used to develop a team. The Level 2 course is two days long and costs $117.70 (incl. GST).

NCCP Level 3
The NCCP Level 3 course is designed to help coaches in their development of team systems. It provides coaches with information on team offense, transition offense, press offense and team defensive strategies. This is a two day course costs $128.40 (incl. GST) and includes coaching seminars from the top basketball coaches in British Columbia.

(www.basketball.bc.ca)

Canada's programs use one certification for each age level; meanwhile, certifications offered by various United States sports federations move from general (Level I) to specific (Level III+). The Levels are not specific to one age group; Level I provides the basics each coach requires and Level III offers a more advanced understanding of specific information. For instance, in the USATF Level I curriculum, one page is devoted to climate considerations and proper hydration strategies on hot days; at Level III, an entire clinic is devoted to climate considerations and training.

Coaching education programs emphasize a safe training environment based on sound scientific principles. Coaching education programs cannot teach coaching; experience and trial and error help a coach improve his coaching. However, a scientific basis and deeper understanding of the sport quickens the learning curve and offers the necessary resources to develop into a better coach.

The following is a brief outline for the Basketball Coaches Training Program. The model more closely resembles the USATF model, as opposed to the Basketball Canada model. While Canada's model provides information valuable to a novice coach, the real deficiency in training in the United States is not a lack of fundamental knowledge, but a misunderstanding or disregard of various scientific principles which underlie basketball development. In the two-day format of the clinics described below, the first day closely parallels the first day of the USATF Clinic outlined above, while the second day is more in-line with the certification programs offered in Canada.

Level I
Eligibility: All Coaches
Format: A two-day seminar offered throughout the year, but especially on weekends in October.
Objective: Introduce new coaches to the basics of risk management, injury prevention, biomechanics and fundamentals; provide a basic scientific background for basketball coaches; create a forum for coaches to get together and discuss basketball; and introduce basic teaching principles and psychological techniques.

Level II
Eligibility: Any coach with a Level I certification and one season of coaching experience.
Format: A two-day seminar; each seminar features a focus for youth, high school or college and is directed towards coaches at these levels.
Objective: Enhance teaching practices of experienced coaches; provide an outlet for continued education; focus coaches on development aspects pertaining to the ages (genders) they coach; provide a more in-depth look at the science of training, especially with respect to periodization and injury prevention; and elevate the precision of fundamental teaching instruction and communication.

Level III
Eligibility: Any coach with a Level II certification and five years of coaching experience.
Format: Participation at two two-day advanced seminars.
Objective: Train master coaches to present at Level I and II clinics; create a standard of excellence for elite coaches; prepare coaches for coaching elite athletes, whether youth, high school or college; present coaches with training concepts on and off the court; and elevate the level of coaching and training on a national level.

Some topics covered during the three-level curriculum:

Philosophy, Ethics and Risk Management
Athlete-centered
Emphasize learning, fun and development
Age-appropriate exercises
Off-court legal issues

Physiology
Anaerobic vs. aerobic conditioning

Periodization
Strength Training for Basketball

Biomechanics
Proper running, jumping, stopping and landing form
Injury prevention (especially ACLs)

Biomotor Training
Introduce five biomotor qualities: Strength, Speed, Flexibility, Endurance and Coordination
Explain each as it relates to basketball

Psychology
Goal Setting
Empowering athletes
Nurturing confidence
Relaxation breathing
Visualization

      The second day consists of on-court instruction, focusing on basic fundamentals, proper execution of fundamentals and each participant leading small groups to work on a training style; as part of the USA Weightlifting course, each participant instructed one lift to the group, and through the learning process of each lift, we worked in pairs helping and teaching each other.

      In the absence of coaching education programs and guidance, coaches train with the Peak by Friday mentality and fail to consider the best interests of the developing athlete. Most coaching clinics focus on basketball tactics; if a speaker tackles a subject other than set plays or defensive rotations or press breaks, the room empties. Coaches devour basketball DVDs on zone offense and run and jump presses, but do little to expand their knowledge in basics like running and jumping biomechanics.

      A certification does not necessarily make someone a good coach. Coaching, to a large degree, depends on one's intangibles and personality, such as building trust and rapport with players, communicating effectively, setting appropriate expectations, reading player's personalities and adjusting or accommodating accordingly, and more. However, a solid understanding of the basics outlined above is equally important; maintaining a safe environment, training to prevent serious injuries, using appropriate exercises, implementing appropriate conditioning and strength programs, training players' mental ability, etc.

      Completing a certification may not insure every coach understands all the concepts outlined above, and others included in the curriculum, but for coaches truly interested in bettering their coaching ability and assisting their athletes, this curriculum provides the basics for a coach to expand his personal horizons and challenge himself/herself to learn more or improve his/her weaknesses. Beyond gaining experience, watching games, talking with other coaches, working camps and other ways to improve one's coaching, a certification process and the curriculum it covers offers industrious coaches another manner to improve their coaching ability and level of knowledge in an efficient manner.

Chapter 11:
Introduction to a New Youth System

For generations, schools served as the primary sponsor of athletic teams, though various organizations sponsor youth leagues (AYSO, Little League, Police Athletic Leagues). In the last twenty to thirty years, businessmen and the major shoe companies changed the entire basketball landscape, shifting importance away from the school season and creating a mammoth uncontrolled, unregulated off-season circuit designed almost entirely to expose players to college coaches, introduce top players to particular shoe brands and clothe these players in free gear.

According to several college coaches, their staffs attend, on average, between forty and sixty high school basketball games per season and 400 to 750 AAU/club games during the spring, summer and fall evaluation periods; college coaches attend 2-3 tournaments with 40-50 teams filled with legitimate college prospects rather than one high school basketball game. These exposure events masquerade as competitive games, though they merely showcase players for college coaches and scouts. Borderline players travel to as many showcase events and tournaments as logistics allow, ignoring practice time and individual workouts that could improve the player's skills or physical attributes, which would increase their value to college programs.

Players covet the college scholarship, so they chase the elusive dream through the spring, summer and fall; meanwhile, high school programs create off-season club programs to keep teams together year-round and fight club coaches for players' allegiances and time.

Without any unifying concept, each team operates individually, which contributes to numerous problems inherent in the current hodge-podge system:

1) Teams/coaches fight for players' allegiance and time, whether the high school team and AAU team compete for players' off-season commitment, AAU team fights AAU team for top players or high schools recruit the top prospects.
2) Players play too many games: 30-35 games in the high school season; 40-60 games with the high school in the off-season; and 30-50 games with an AAU team.
3) Each season is an end in and of itself; no level looks at itself as a developmental level, as each team fights for the league, section, regional or national championship. Teams train to win as youths, rather than preparing players gradually for intense competition.
4) Eleven year olds suffer overuse injuries such as tendonitis, plantar fasciitis or shin splints.
5) No consistency. One coach teaches a concept one way, while the player's coach the next season teaches it differently; even worse, one coach employs several set plays and allocates a significant percentage of training time toward memorization and execution of plays, and the coach the next year runs different plays and allocates a significant portion of training toward execution of his plays. From season to season, players spend more time memorizing new plays as opposed to learning to play basketball.

The system fails to develop better players or maximize their individual potential. High school programs lack flexibility and are a small part of the overall academic mission within a school; in an interview at a local public school the Vice Principal asked two of seventeen questions about basketball and/or coaching. High school coaches are teachers first and coaches second. Elite athletes require nurturing and development beyond the means of the typical high school. Accelerated students in many districts take community college classes to complete the required curriculum. In essence, these students seek academic opportunities beyond their school.

Many talented players seek club basketball opportunities to improve their game and gain college exposure. The scholarship quest requires more and more exposure, which means more travel and more games, leaving less time for individual practice, skill instruction and athletic development. Many players peak around sixteen years old because they start early and play frequently; they master skills, though often incorrectly.

Eric Kravitz, a graduate student from Philadelphia, examined the differences between the Italian and American basketball systems and wrote:

> One of the most influential differences between the Italian and American development styles involves the overall aims of the institutions. In Italy with the domestic clubs serving as both the training and professional levels of development there tends to be more of a long-term approach towards winning, as most clubs have the ability to be patient with their younger players. While enjoyable when it happens, the youth teams are not designed to actually win, but rather develop players for the more senior teams…Therefore, regardless of age or their initial inherent skill level, all youth players within a club system are instructed in the same fundamental basketball skills for the entire development period…Without immediate pressure to win, Italian youth teams and players are free to explore various developmental strategies in order to best help players grow. Thereby, in making winning secondary, Italian club teams enable their coaching and training staff to focus on the primary goal of developing talented and fundamentally complete players…In America the institutions responsible for player development are typically constrained by a short-term model.

A youth coach's focus should be development and learning; youth sport is preparation for further athletic participation, whether recreational or competitive. This preparation is physical and mental, general and sport-specific.

Instead, athletes spend thousands of dollars chasing the ephemeral dream. I asked 20-25 random parents about the expense of AAU involvement. Respondents spent anywhere from $600 to $12,000 a year for club fees, uniforms, tournaments, travel, etc, and most placed the sum between $2000-$5000 per year. It was not uncommon for parents to drive an hour each way two to three times a week for practice in addition to traveling to weekend tournaments. While the truly elite or well-connected play on shoe-sponsored teams without expense, the majority of high school players spend thousands pursuing the college dream.

Coaches, players and parents ignore the most important aspect of the college scholarship process: the player must have the talent, skills and potential to warrant a scholarship offer. Otherwise, exposure is not going to get the player a full ride. Unfortunately, AAU/club basketball may not aid development, as "The individual development is lacking at the AAU level," according to one West Coast Conference Assistant Coach.

While the best players are great with the ball in their hands, they lack the wherewithal to play a team game within a coach's system. Players stand and watch without the ball and lack the feel for the game. They reach, lunge for steals and do not understand help defense and defensive rotations.

The shoe-sponsored AAU and exposure camp system disrupts development at every level, and the game deteriorates aesthetically, as fewer players understand the game's nuances or possess fundamental skills. Instead of a well-organized, year-round program to mesh the strengths of AAU and high school basketball, players go from the train to win high school season to the exposure-dominated AAU season, while coaches bicker and fight. Nowhere is the goal improvement, learning, fun or individual development and different coaches fail to communicate and cooperate.

As another Big West Conference Assistant Coach said, "I would say that this process has added a lot of stress to a group of kids that range between 15 and 17 years of age. Now kids pay a tremendous amount of money to play ball for three weeks in the summer. They do not get to practice the game or develop skills during that time...Sometimes, especially at the end of the July period, when kids are tired to the bone and play is really sloppy I truly wonder and wish kids are having a good time on the court and enjoying the game. I think sometimes we lose sight of that."

Basketball in the United States needs a better model to develop and nurture these talents. Sneaker pimps stripped away the innocence and purity once associated with high school athletics, and a revolutionary change is needed to advance basketball development and create a more fun, equitable and efficient means for developing elite players and providing more recreational opportunities for adolescents and teenagers.

In the last five years, the English FA (Football Association) concluded it needed a better way to develop the next generation of English soccer talent. The FA's Technical Department researched training methods, examined its current system and concluded several areas needed to be addressed in an effort to maximize its young players' potential, maintain the Premiere League's status as arguably the top league in the world and keep the English National Team among the world's elite.

The FA developed a model to guide elite player development and address the following six issues:

1. Elite young players require a development process to protect and nurture their special talents.
2. Technical development cannot and should not be viewed in isolation of the player's overall educational and social welfare.
3. FA Premiere League and Football League Clubs need to have more access to the very best players.
4. Young gifted players are exposed to too much competitive football and too little practice time.
5. Competitive matches are part of an integrated development program.
6. Better qualified coaches to work with elite young players.

(theFA.com)

In an effort to maximize the basketball talents of the United States' best and brightest young players, USA Basketball, the NBA and those that care about basketball development must address the FA's issues as an initial assessment of the current state of American basketball and its future.

1. Elite young players require a development process to protect and nurture their special talents.

Currently, the United States has no plan governing the development of its young athletes. Athletes develop in a survival of the fittest environment with little guidance or direction offered by experienced, knowledgeable mentors/organizations. This book examines this issue from cover to cover.

2. Technical development cannot and should not be viewed in isolation of the player's overall educational and social welfare.

In Spain, select individuals join Player Development Centers where "the goal is to help basketball players between fourteen and eighteen years of age train in the most efficient way so basketball is compatible with their studies and personal development," (Sergio). The Centers exist to train elite players through an organized development plan which focuses on three aspects: "physical, psychological and technical-tactical," (Sergio).

In today's basketball system, players play year-round with two teams and often train with a personal trainer to get the individual technical instruction absent in many team practices. Players fatigue, burn out and expend tremendous energy pursuing basketball; dozens of players each year forfeit college scholarships because they do not meet NCAA minimum standards. The chaotic, year-round system creates conflict within a young person's life. A more organized, efficient model would benefit players on and off the court.

3. Professional access to the very best players.

In the FA, each Premiere League and Football League club sponsors an elite player development Academy for players who live within an hour's drive of the club. The 39 Academies feature six full-time, qualified coaches and trainers.

No integrated development system exists in the Unite States. The NBA Player's Association sponsors a camp for 50-100 boys each year and USA Basketball conducts its annual basketball festival to select players for various junior teams, but no systematic, year-round program exists. When NCAA institutions or NBA teams sponsor programs, they aim for the lower-end player; camps and clinics are little more than glorified day care and extended autograph sessions. USA Basketball can apply band-aid solutions to the problems of 2002 and 2004, like hiring Jerry Colangelo and Coach K, but if it wants to secure sustained success, an Academy model is the surest way to insure gold is again an American basketball player's birthright.

4. Young gifted players are exposed to too much competitive football and too little practice time.

The English Academies limit players to a maximum of thirty games a year, a far cry from the 100+ games an elite high school basketball player plays. The English Academies limit players under twelve years of age to small-sided games, with no full 11-a-side matches; in the USA, six year olds play full court 5v5 games in basketball leagues.

Competition is essential to growth and development; however, balance between training and competition is necessary. Elite players' hectic schedules sacrifice individual work, resistance training, normal teenage activities, family vacations, rest or regeneration. Players compete year-round in a semi-professional environment with pressure to perform. Without proper rest, bodies wear out and performance decreases due to overtraining and over-competing.

The box below is the training schedule of the Newcastle United u-18 Academy as supplied by Adrian Lamb, the Strength and Conditioning Coach for the Newcastle United Football Academy. This schedule offers an idea as to the schedule of other elite athletes; athletic skills training (weights and speed/plyos) receive almost equal emphasis as technical training, while the match and match preparation receive less emphasis. Even with the u-18 sides, development is emphasized over competition.

Newcastle United Football Academy u-18's Training Schedule

Mon: 9:30-10:45 Weights; 10:45-12:30 Technical training
Tues: 10:00-10:30 Speed/plyos; 10:30-12:00 Technical training
Wed: 10:30-12:30 Technical training 2:30-3:45 Weights
Thurs: off
Fri: Match Preparation
Sat: Match
Sun: Recovery

---

5. Competitive matches are part of an integrated development program.

Within the framework of a planned development model, players must measure themselves and their progress against other teams and players. Games increase motivation and give players a goal. When rowing in college, the toughest part was training for six months before our first meaningful race. Games are an essential component of the development model; however, make each game important and competitive to elicit both teams' best effort.

Competition derives from the Latin root "to seek together." Evenly matched, well-played games elevate the level of each performer/team. For young athletes, competition is not about winning, but performing to one's potential and testing one's newly acquired skills in competition. Competition-win or lose- should be fun, not cause stress or panic. Players should not play with a fear of failure or anxiety. Competition is healthy, but the "will to win must come from within the child. Parents, activity leaders and trainers must only create conditions, through organizing matches and giving training sessions, in keeping with the perceived world of the child," (Michels).

6. Better qualified coaches to work with elite young players.

Anyone can start their own AAU or club basketball team and volunteer fathers coach many youth school teams; this does not guarantee a bad experience or a poor coach, but it certainly does not insure a qualified coach. As a WCC Assistant Coach said: "Lastly, I'll say there are 3 types of AAU coaches: 1) He/she does it to make money. Their number one priority is to use kids to make money. 2) He/she does it for ego. They want to talk to college coaches, have coaches kissing their butt to get a kid and feel like they are more important than they probably are. 3) He/she does it because they want to see the kids improve, they want to help the kids get exposure and they do it for the right reasons." Fewer and fewer coaches fall into category number three.

Developmentally, the most important years are the skill hungry years between seven and fourteen years old, and specifically between ten and twelve years old for basketball-specific skills. While the most experienced, best basketball teachers reside and make millions working in the NBA, novice coaches and parents train players during the crucial periods of development. And, USA Basketball nor the NABC provides coaches training or coaching education programs for these novice coaches who influence the development of the next generation of players.

In 2003, ESPN commentator/writer Jay Bilas wrote:

> No reasonable basketball person can refute the fact that the fundamental skills of American players are slipping, and so is the American game. I believe a primary reason is an increased emphasis on coaching the game, and a decreased emphasis on teaching our kids how to play the game. Pete Newell, the legendary coach and teacher, has often said that basketball is "over-coached and under-taught". He is absolutely right, and that is finally catching up with us, as is the rest of the basketball world...The measure of a teacher is not in winning, but in the fundamental soundness and skill level of the players taught. A player with excellent fundamentals and skills can play successfully in any system...The United States produces the best "athletes" in the game, but not necessarily the best "basketball players".

(America needs more 'teaching' from its coaches, ESPN.com)

If we are committed to developing the next generation of basketball players and maximizing their talent, we must use sports science and the most successful development models. These six areas highlight deficiencies in the current system. The entire sports culture needs a new approach, critical thinking and a science-based plan. By rushing development in pursuit of junior national championships and high school victories, we short-change the elite athlete, who peaks early in his career, and the non-elite athlete, who lacks exposure to a variety of activities. A long term athletic development model serves the interests of the elite and non-elite athlete, while the current American development system fails everyone.

Chapter 12:
The Elite Development League and Elite+

The Elite Development League concept aims to maximize player development in an efficient manner through a partnership between the NBA/NBDL and USA Basketball. Each NBA team adopts or starts a local basketball academy, creating 39 academies throughout the United States. Additionally, cities without NBA teams could start similar academies and join the EDL if it meets the EDL requirements. Academies would enroll a minimum of one hundred high school-aged players each. Athletes would attend high school as normal, but the Academy would provide all necessary training services, from a licensed nutritionist to a strength coach to basketball coaches to academic tutors. Money to support these academies would come from NBA teams and a television deal with ESPN to televise several games and the annual national championship. The Academy model meets the needs of elite athletes who need a more efficient means to train and develop; colleges benefit because local coaches narrow the talent pool through selection to the academies.

Many American high school soccer players forsake high school soccer for better opportunities, better coaching and more talented teammates in club soccer, which offers a more competitive and advanced training environment. In high school soccer, many elite players are unchallenged, especially at practice, where training is geared toward the average player, not the elite. The Elite Development League creates a similar, competitive training environment for American basketball players in a unified model. High school basketball would exist, giving more opportunities to players who want to play sports, not be consumed by year-round practices and tournaments. The EDL would be like D-I sports, while high school teams would be more like D-III sports.

The EDL is similar to the Premiere League Academies. Rather than players playing with high school teams and club teams, playing over 100 games a year and being pulled in several directions by other people's interests, the EDL centralizes elite player development. The NBA and NBDL partnership with the EDL would include use of professional training facilities; access to professional coaches, trainers and strength coaches; low athlete to instructor ratio; and access to latest technology.

The EDL would provide academic support, on-court training, strength and speed training, nutrition advice and the best training environment available in the world. The EDL would provide a more efficient means of player development and replace the conflicts and competition between high schools and clubs. Hopefully, the EDL would curb high school recruiting and allow high school students the opportunity to attend classes with friends, not worry about attending a certain school for its basketball program. Most games occur during basketball season, so players could participate in other school sports if they choose. The goal in professionalizing the system is to allow teenagers a more normal life, while also supporting, developing and nurturing their natural athletic gifts.

Canada realized it needed a new approach and four years ago developed its first regional training center.

The Canada Basketball Nike - Centre for Performance-British Columbia (CP-BC) is an elite development program designed to teach players individual and team offensive fundamentals. It also introduces aspects of sports science that are necessary to the development of elite level players and coaches. The CP-BC program is a key component of Canada Basketball's strategy to identify and develop national team players and coaches.

The Nike CP-BC program was established four years ago in British Columbia under the name Regional Training Centre (RTC). It was developed because of the recognition that B.C. athletes needed access to a program that integrated consistent fundamental skill development, highly qualified coaching and elite level competition. The Nike CP-BC program offers a highly qualified coaching staff using a curriculum developed by Canada Basketball to work with participants aged between 12 to 18 years.

The program curriculum has a heavy emphasis on developing individual offensive fundamentals and also teaches team principles of play. Players take part in seminars and receive information on sports nutrition, mental training, strength, agility and physical testing using nationally developed standards. In addition, through the use of the Nike CP-BC program training diaries, athletes are taught time management and planning skills. (www.basketball.bc.ca)

These Centers for Performance offer an excellent model for each individual Academy, as the Academy's goal is not simply to win games, but maximize the overall talents of its players through an integrated, systematic approach. The basics of the Academies are outlined below:

EDL Academy
- Train 3-4 days a week.
- Basketball training, strength training and conditioning.
- Supply nutrition information.
- Provide sports psychology training.
- Utilize state of the art facilities.
- Field multiple teams to accommodate all its payers and insure each player receives sufficient playing time.

EDL Format
- Divide into four conferences, north, south, east and west for each level/team.
- Play the other conference members in a home and home series; roughly an 18 game schedule.
- The conference champions meet in April in a Final Four.
- For exposure, a cup championship: the EDL sponsors a Thanksgiving Tournament, Christmas Tournament, Spring Break Tournament (recruiting window) and an Independence Day Tournament. Teams compete in 2 tournaments, adding another 4-10 games to the schedule.
- The Cup Championship invites the semi-finalists from each tournament to the EDL Classic during the final week in July.

- Maximum games played if a team went undefeated and won the Final Four Championship, 2 tournament championships and the Classic, would be 37 games or roughly the same number as a college team.

EDL Coaches
- Primary job is athlete development, not wins.
- Work closely with other athletic personnel-strength coaches, athletic trainers, etc.-to insure each player's health and development
- Create a manageable long term schedule to maximize the player's ability.
- Evaluated on ability to work with other athletic personnel, long term planning and overall development of basketball skills for the Academy players.
- Hire the best coaches for these positions because of the developmental importance during this age period.

Elite+ Program

Beyond the EDL, the Elite+ Program mimics US Soccer's Project 40, part of US Soccer's Project 2010 which originated as an organized plan to build a national team capable of winning the 2010 World Cup.

> Project 40 is aimed at providing America's top young talent with the valuable training needed to develop their skills and further the United States' international success…the program's more specific goal is to provide each player with the opportunity to participate in as many quality matches as possible, enabling the player to develop at an accelerated pace during the crucial ages of 17-22.

> Project-40 players earn the minimum annual MLS salary during their initial season and are awarded a five-year academic package covering tuition. In most cases, each MLS team will have one to three Project-40 players on their roster. These players do not count against the club's 20-man roster.

> Nowhere was the development of quality U.S. youth soccer players more evident than at the 2002 World Cup, in which Project-40 graduates Landon Donovan and DaMarcus Beasley, starting for the U.S. at the age of 20, emerged on the world's top stage along with the likes of fellow Pro-40 graduate Josh Wolff.

> (US Soccer web page)

Elite+ Program Players
- Sign and play with nearest NBDL team; forfeit college eligibility.
- Become draft eligible after one full season in the NBDL.
- Continue Academy participation around the NBDL schedule.
- Earn a minimum contract.
- Receive academic support to insure players finish high school diploma and have a financial package to attend college.
- Play in EDL tournaments around the NBDL schedule.
- Participate in one NBA Rookie Summer League/Camp.
- Open to the truly elite players like LeBron James, Dwight Howard, etc who are surefire #1 draft picks; no minimum or maximum number per year. A consensus of NBA scouts nominates players and the players choose to join the Elite+ Program or remain with the EDL. Players who want to go to college remain with Academy full-time.

The Elite+ program (and to a certain extent the EDL) solves five major problems facing basketball:

1. The NCAA rules curtailing the practice time of college players with their coaches.
2. Universities dubious role as a minor league system and the perpetual investigations, improprieties and violations created and manipulated by the system.
3. High school recruiting (and high school budget cuts limiting access and funding for teams).
4. The need for a minor league to prepare professional players.
5. The need for American players to develop a greater skill level and not to learn to rely on natural talent until they reach the NBA.

As sports' competitiveness grows, sports federations must evolve to meet players' changing needs. What worked a generation ago is out-dated. American basketball must move forward to meet new challenges and provide a better system of player development for young players.

When training athletes, the primary goal is injury prevention/reduction; second is performance enhancement. Many programs do a static stretch as a team because tradition dictates stretching before playing a sport. However, science suggests otherwise. According to a Japanese study published in the *Journal of Strength and Conditioning*, "Research found that static stretching has no positive effect on muscular performance," (*Men's Health*, December 2005).

A dynamic warm-up prepares the athlete for training and trains fundamental movement skills. Static stretching-the traditional reach and hold stretch- is insufficient to prepare an athlete for quick, powerful movements associated with sports. "Because convincing scientific evidence supporting the injury-reducing and performance enhancing potential of static stretching is presently lacking, it may be desirable for children to perform dynamic exercise during the warm-up period and static during the cool down period," (Faigenbaum, et al.).

"The main physiological reason for a warm up include; to increase core temperature (an increase in rectal temperature of a least one to two degree Celsius appears to be sufficient); to increase heart rate and blood flow to skeletal tissues, which improves the efficiency of oxygen uptake and transport, carbon dioxide removal, and removal and breakdown of anaerobic byproducts (lactate); to increase the activation of the Central Nervous System (therefore increasing co-ordination, skill accuracy and reaction time); to increase the rate and force of muscle contraction and contractile mechanical efficiency (through increased muscle temperature), and to increase the suppleness of connective tissue (resulting in less incidence of musculotendonous injuries).

The result of the above responses lead to an athlete's increased ability to do physical work, which is extremely important for sports requiring short duration high intensity work bursts such as sprinting and jumping. The improvement in the nervous system is especially helpful for athletes involved in sports that demand high levels of complete body movement, such as team sport athletes." (http://www.elitetrack.com/articles/warmup.pdf)

Injuries often occur in sports because the body is ill-prepared for the intensity of the movement; either the warm-up failed to elevate the muscle temperature and loosen the muscle or the movement exceeded the athlete's normal range of motion; training the full range of motion in warm-ups, not just jogging, is important to insure sports preparedness.

A Dynamic Warm-up can include some or all of these exercises, depending on the goal and time allotment. However, as the primary warm-up for practice or competition, use several different exercises that hit different muscle groups.

Basic Warm-up (down/back)

- Jog/Backpedal
- Toe Walk/Heel Walk
- Monkey Shuffle [shuffle with arm swing; hands cross in front of body and extend above shoulders]
- Crossover Step [like half carioca; when moving R-L, right foot steps in front of left foot, left foot steps out and then right foot in front of left again]
- Half-Speed/Backpedal
- Skip/Backward Skip
- Lunge/Step-over [lift leg and open hips, like stepping over a small hurdle]
- Three-quarter Speed/Back pedal
- Carioca
- Frankenstein Walk [straight leg march; put hands straight out in front and kick your foot to your hands]/Butt Kicks
- Full Speed/Backpedal
- 45-degree bound
- Hand Walk [start in push-up position; walk feet to hands; walk out hands; repeat]
- Full Speed/Backpedal

Additional Exercises

- Ankling [keep feet dorsiflexed; run with feet stepping over the opposite ankle]
- Squat
- Side to Side Hops
- Jump Rope Exercises
- Lateral Skip
- Straight Leg Running [kick legs out in front]
- Exaggerated Stride Skip [kick heel to butt and extend leg]
- Side Lunge
- Drop Squat [starting in an athletic stance, move your left leg behind and to the right of your right leg; squat]
- Scorpion [Lie on stomach, so body forms a T. Keep your arms still, thrust left heel toward right hand]
- Frog [Push-up position; punch knees to chest; feet land in between elbows; push legs back to starting position]
- Mountain Climber

References

Baechle, Thomas and Earle, Roger. (2000). Essentials of Strength and Conditioning. Champaign, IL: Human Kinetics. (pp. 17-20, 83-88).

Balyi, Dr. Istvan. "Sport system building and long term athlete development in Canada-The Situation and the Solutions." *Coaches Report*, vol. 8, summer 2001.

Balyi, Dr. Istvan and Hamilton, Ann. "Long-Term Athlete Development: Traininability in Childhood and Adolesence Windows of Opportunity, Optimal Trainability." May, 2003.

Bompa, Tudor O. (2000). Total Training for Young Champions. Champaign, IL: Human Kinetics.

Boyle, Michael. (2004). Functional Training for Sports. Champaign, IL: Human Kinetics.

Coakley, Jay. (2001). Sport in Society. San Francisco: McGraw Hill.

Chek, Paul. (2000). Movement that Matters. Encinitas, CA: C.H.E.K. Institute.

Damon, William. (1995). Greater Expectations. New York: Free Press Paperbacks.

Douillard, John. (1994). Body, Mind, and Sport. New York: Three Rivers Press.

Gambetta, Vern. (2002). Gambetta Method. Sarasota, Fl: Gambetta Sports Training Systems, Inc.

Grasso, Brian J. (2005). Training Young Athletes-The Grasso Method. Developing Athletics Inc.

Launder, Alan G. (2001). Play Practice. Champaign, IL: Human Kinetics.

Michels, Rinus. (2001). Teambuilding the Road to Success. Spring City, PA: Reedswain Publishing.

Oliver, Dean. (2004). Basketball on Paper. Washington, D.C.: Brassey's Inc.

Sergio, Carlos. "The Spanish Basketball Federation Youth Program." *FIBA Assist Magazine*. Winter, 2003

Thanks to Mike MacKay, Manager Coach Education and Development, Canada Basketball and Adrian Lamb, Strength and Conditioning Coach for the Newcastle United Football Academy for responding to inquiries and assisting with information.

About the Author

Brian McCormick resides in Sacramento, California where he trains youth, high school and college basketball players. After completing a B.A. in American Literature at UCLA, directing the UCLA Special Olympics program and rowing for the UCLA Crew team, McCormick coached as a men's assistant coach at UC Santa Cruz and a women's assistant coach at Santa Monica College before moving to Sweden as the Head Coach of the Visby Ladies in Sweden's Damligan (professional women's league). Additionally, McCormick worked with the Visby AIK youth programs in Sweden and assisted at Brentwood School, Mt. Hood Community College, Hoop Masters and the Santa Monica Surf and coached volleyball and basketball at Notre Dame Academy in West Los Angeles.

McCormick is a Certified Strength and Conditioning Specialist through the National Strength and Conditioning Association; Sports Performance Coach through USA Weightlifting; Level I Coach through USA Track and Field and a Johnny G certified Spinning instructor. He completed a Master's in Sports Science through the United States Sports Academy.

McCormick is the author of three books: The Art of Ball Handling: Getting a Handle on Your Game; Pure: The Biomechanics and Mental Approach to Successful Shooting; and Hard 2 Guard: The Fundamental Skills of the Unstoppable Perimeter Player. He is an Associate Editor with *Basketball Sense* and his articles have appeared in magazines in South Africa, Canada and Italy.

McCormick operates a message board for interested coaches: (http://hoopstraining.proboards74.com) and can be reached via email at highfivehoopschool@yahoo.com.

Made in the USA
Lexington, KY
20 January 2011